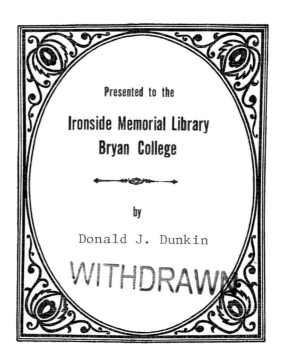

HELP WANTED: FAITH REQUIRED

BY William Proctor

SURVIVAL ON THE CAMPUS
HELP WANTED: FAITH REQUIRED

HELP WANTED: FAITH REQUIRED

William Proctor

Fleming H. Revell Company
Old Tappan, New Jersey

Library of Congress Cataloging in Publication Data

Proctor, William.
    Help wanted: faith required.

    1.   Labor and laboring classes—Religious life.
2.   Business ethics.   I.   Title.
BV4593.P76   248'.88   73-19534
ISBN 0-8007-0642-0

TO
my wife, Pam,
who has always been my best critic

Contents

Preface

Do You Thank God It's Monday?

We all know the symptoms—a foggy brain, dragging feet, a general sense of depression at the sight of the breakfast cereal. These are the classic signs of that age-old working-man's malady, the Monday morning blues. At one time or another we've all uttered a complaint that's associated with this sickness: "They're working me to the bone . . . everybody cheats, so why not me? . . . all work and no play . . . a woman's work is never done . . . it's all such a bore . . . what's it all for? . . . if only I had a million dollars."

But it's not necessary for the good spirits and moral standards of working people to be trampled by dissatisfaction, boredom, and anxiety. God has provided a way to overcome the occupational doldrums, to go beyond that exhausted, disillusioned cry, "Thank God it's Friday!" Given an opportunity, he can provide us with the enthusiasm to declare instead, "Thank God it's Monday and Tuesday and Wednesday!"

But how, exactly, can we find this sense of meaning and satisfaction at work? First of all, we have to focus on God and not on any particular job. The basic mistake of most workers, Christian and non-Christian alike, is that they seek ultimate job fulfillment only within the narrow confines of their daily tasks. I've never encountered anyone whose job

9

could fulfill such lofty expectations. Because we can't expect any occupation, by itself, to give our lives a complete sense of purpose, we should try bringing God to work with us each morning.

Jesus of Nazareth realized that most people would prefer to put God on a convenient little shelf during the week until they're ready to take him out for a weekly religious observance. Human beings are, by nature, hesitant to release any control over their livelihood and earning capacity. They're afraid that if God and his moral demands get mixed up with their careers, they may lose promotions or impair their financial security. But Christ was quite explicit in reminding us that any commitment to him must be total. If we want to experience his power, we can't make him Lord of only one part of our lives.

There are an appalling number of Christians who assume God is not interested in their careers. They live as though he is too tired to commute with them each morning, or too busy to put in a full day next to them on their daily chores. When I mentioned to friends that I was working on a book on the application of the Christian faith to the business world, a typical response would be, "Oh, is that going to be a book with blank pages?" Or, "I guess that should be a pretty short volume—maybe ten pages or so?"

These quips were made half in jest, but they were also half-serious. The unspoken assumption was, "Sure, God calls some people to be preachers and some to be missionaries. But they've been given a special vocation for full-time Christian service. As for me, I'm a banker [or construction worker, or homemaker]. Just so long as I keep my nose fairly clean and make a decent living for my family, God's not going to get interested in the petty details of my working life."

But God won't let us limit him this way. He is at least as interested in our work as in our leisure activities, because we spend most of our time on the job. To exclude God from our occupations is to exclude him from most of our existence.

During the past few years I've found a number of Christians who have risen above the pressures and concerns of their daily jobs and perceived a basic occupational truth: God *can* act at work. Faith can turn a frustrating day into a satisfying lesson, or an abrasive relationship into a productive friendship. These Christians' experiences, some of which are described in the following pages as composite events, demonstrate concrete ways for us to take our faith to work. The men and women in these incidents come from every walk of life—executives, tradesmen, professionals, secretaries, and homemakers. I hope, as you examine their encounters with God at work, you'll find spiritual inspirations and techniques which will enrich your own career.

HELP WANTED: FAITH REQUIRED

1
The Fundamentals of Working a Christian Life

Everyone gets disillusioned with his job at one time or another. In those periods of depression we can usually identify with the ancient Hebrew preacher's pessimism about the workingman: ". . . all his days are full of pain, and his work is a vexation; even in the night his mind does not rest" (Ecclesiastes 2:23).

But a job doesn't have to be like that, for Jesus said, "I came that they may have life, and have it abundantly" (John 10:10). The first step in finding this abundant life at work is to understand three simple, but fundamental principles of working a Christian life.

Principle 1. God has called you to be a Christian at work.

As obvious as this statement may seem, far too many of us fit the classic image of the "Sunday Christians" who give God his dues at Sunday worship services and then leave him behind at the commuter-train stop on Monday morning. Some working people, however, have found that God operates as well in an office or factory as he does in a church.

The Christian faith can provide "a moral freshness, like a

stream of air in a stale room, that inspires us to maintain high ethical standards on the job," Dr. Ralph Minear, a Boston pediatrician, observed. "When I'm at work, I try to keep foremost in my mind the Christian values of helping and loving my fellow man. And as a physician, I get great satisfaction from knowing that my medical skills can give me the power to express love to those who are sick or needy."

Minear thus accentuates the personal side of work, instead of dwelling exclusively on such impersonal factors as putting out a certain work product or achieving a high level of efficiency. One of the Christian's greatest challenges on the job is to achieve proficiency without overlooking the humanity of co-workers, bosses, and subordinates.

For Ralph Filicchia, an employee in a Boston rigging firm, the impact of a Christian commitment at work "can be wrapped up in four words: 'Be a nice guy.' That's what it's all about. Of course, there's a lot of theology behind being a nice guy, because you have to let Christ live through you.

"It's all spelled out in some of Paul's Epistles: being kind, courteous, loving, doing unto others. But if you wanted to summarize them, you'd say, 'Be a nice guy.' I know a lot of Christians who live as though some of those verses were not in the Bible. God wants us to know the Scriptures, but I don't think he's in the business of making minitheologians. He's in the business of making nice guys. For me, to become a nice guy is much more important than knowing the different theories on how the world is going to end.

"If you can't get along with other people, you haven't graduated from spiritual kindergarten. I see people who call themselves Christians yelling at others to shut up. That's incredible. To me, worldliness—the opposite of godliness—

is screaming out of a window at another driver as I'm traveling from one job to the next, or making a fool out of someone in a union meeting. Or it's gossiping about my fellow workers. That's what a worldly guy would do, but not a nice guy, not a Christian."

Being a nice guy and stressing the personal are simply concrete ways of saying that the Christian must lead a transformed life on the job, as well as in nonworking activities. The committed Christian keeps in touch with God through prayer and relies on the Spirit of God to give him a sensitivity to the needs of others; his personality at work is constantly being conformed to the moral outline of Christ.

Principle 2. God may not call you to one special career.

A few people believe that God has called them to one particular job. One physician I know was certain, from his high-school years, that he wanted to be a doctor. Without veering in the slightest through college and medical school, he became a dedicated internist. He felt he would have been subverting God's will if he had pursued another career.

A similar idea was expressed by Bob Goode, a New Jersey high-school teacher who specializes in science. "I have a calling in the sense that I really feel I belong in my teaching job," he explained. "It's not like a bolt out of the blue, but my job is a place where I fit in quite naturally. I sense a God-given responsibility to reform education, to prevent school from being a grim and joyless experience. I want to make it a place where kids come alive, where learning and thinking are encouraged."

But other Christians, especially those in dull, routine jobs, have a completely different attitude. "This thing about God having a wonderful career plan for your life I consider to be complete rubbish," one construction worker declared. "I see nothing in the Bible to back that up. I don't think God cares whether I'm a butcher or baker or candlestick maker. The will of God for my life is to be conformed to the image of Christ, period."

One woman who has had a string of secretarial and clerical jobs expressed similar sentiments. "I was always told that God had a plan for my life, a comprehensive design, and I took it for granted that this meant a career pattern. I assumed this divine pattern would bring me fulfillment, but every job has been, in the end, a disappointment.

"So I started blaming myself: What am I doing wrong? Why am I unable to understand God's purpose for me? Now I'm beginning to realize it's wrong to get so obsessed with finding a job that will bring me the abundant life. Jesus himself was just a carpenter, but who thinks about him that way now? His trade wasn't the central thing about his life. And Paul was an educated man, of the intellectual class, yet he made tents for a living. As for me, I'm a typist, even though I have some college training. But my education isn't being wasted, because I use it as a church-school teacher."

Ila Lee Miller, an educator and administrator in nonprofit organizations, said she's come to some similar conclusions about her work: "God may lead me to a specific job because there are people there who need me, but usually not because the work itself is so important. Also, I've learned to guard against expecting too much from a secular job. Otherwise, I may overlook the really important tasks God wants me to do, either at church or elsewhere in the Christian community."

Different Christians, then, hold a wide variety of views about how God influences their choice of career. God clearly leads some people into a certain line of work, but his plan for others often doesn't center on a particular daily job. A person can best determine his career role not by casting about anxiously for some divinely preordained occupation, but rather by concentrating on letting Christ live through him, both on and off the job.

Principle 3. Christians rarely get career advice from burning bushes.

One of the first practical problems that confronts the Christian worker is a question that bothers every prospective employee: How should I go about choosing a job and planning a career? Moses, of course, had his career outlined explicitly by God through a voice in a burning bush. But most Christian workers—whether bricklayers, lawyers, or clergymen—don't get such specific guidance. To find their proper career slot, they have to rely on the traditional methods of learning God's will.

David Fuller, a New York attorney, described the procedure this way: "In analyzing a career decision, there's a fairly standard approach to finding God's will: You have to pray, consult the Scriptures, and talk with other people, including other Christians. It's difficult to prove by any objective standard that the positions I've held were definitely the Lord's will. But God has consistently given me an inner confidence that convinces me he's guiding my working life."

Meredith Kattke, an educator from New York, has had comparable experiences in job hunting. Before she went to graduate school and became involved in educational research, Meredith was unsure about what she wanted to do, so she decided to look for a secretarial job to tide her over until she made up her mind. Because she lacked the usual typing and stenographic skills, she was worried at first about making the wrong decision. But after prayer and extensive consultations with a fellow believer, she had an insight: "I realized I couldn't make the wrong decision if I listened for God's direction. He doesn't make mistakes. This was very comforting for me, and I went out looking for a job with a more confident outlook, a feeling of trust and guidance. I did get a good secretarial job, even though I have none of the usual skills, and the money I earned helped me go to graduate school."

These procedures for choosing a job have been used by other Christians, from New Testament days to the present. The initial steps that the first-century Christians took after being baptized, according to Luke's account in Acts 2:42, were to concentrate on three activities: learning from the apostles' teachings, regular associations with other believers, and prayer.

The individual Christian's own intelligence has also always been an important factor in determining the will of God, as the Apostle Paul indicated to his readers in Philippi-ans 2:12. When Paul urged, ". . .work out your own salva-tion with fear and trembling" in that passage, he assumed some human judgment and effort on the part of the individual Christian. In more recent times, the German Protestant minister, Dietrich Bonhoeffer, who was executed by the Nazis in the last days of World War II, also recognized the key role of the intellect in finding the will of God. He wrote in his book *Ethics:* "Intelligence, discernment, attentive observation of the given facts, all these now come into lively operation, all will be embraced and pervaded by prayer."

Because God wants us to use our heads in selecting an appropriate job, one of the first steps in learning God's will is to make a realistic appraisal of our abilities and interests. "I remember deciding that if I did badly on the law-school admission tests or in my work at college, I'd take such failures as an indication that I shouldn't pursue the law as a career," David Fuller explained. "I also talked to people about practicing law, so that I could find out if I'd like the work. As a general principle, there's nothing wrong with a Christian's wanting to enjoy what he's doing. If I didn't enjoy a particular kind of work, then I wouldn't hesitate to choose something else."

Fuller's idea that a Christian has a responsibility to make the best use of his native gifts and interests finds strong support throughout the Scriptures. Jesus, for example, chose a business relationship in Matthew 25:14-30 to illustrate this point. In this parable, a man, in preparing for a lengthy trip, called a meeting of his three workers and entrusted certain portions of his property to their care. When this employer returned to "settle accounts," as Jesus put it, he found that two of the fellows had doubled their money. But the third employee, afraid of the boss who had a reputation for being a "hard man," went and hid the talent in the ground.

The master reprimanded the third worker for his laxity,

saying, ". . . you ought to have invested my money with the bankers, and at my coming I should have received what was my own with interest." And so the tough boss took this man's property away and gave it to the one who had done the best investing job.

Some Christians have decided to limit their job hunting to work which not only fits their talents, but which also has a definite humanitarian purpose. Meredith Kattke said that any job she holds has to be related to "bettering the human condition." She noted that many different jobs could qualify under this occupational test she has set for herself.

"One such job would be the drafting of telephone workers' manuals, which I did in New York City for several months a few summers ago," she said. "I wasn't sure that I wanted to do that, but a former professor had arranged for an interview with the telephone company. My prayer before the interview was, 'Not my will, but thine be done.' I had a right place to be, but I didn't know where it was, and so I trusted God. They offered a good salary, and after I started work I realized I was helping other people. The employees at the company couldn't read the other manuals because they were written at a much higher level than the average metropolitan worker's skill. My job was to simplify the reading level. I feel as though I helped not only the people who had to use the manuals but also those of us who try to telephone. In my view, any work like this is an expression of Christian love, something which betters the human condition."

Summarizing what seems to be the most effective approach for the Christian in career planning, Meredith said, "In choosing a job, you take the human footsteps and realize at the same time that you have to find divine guidance. But understanding God's will is certainly not a matter of hearing a booming voice from heaven or experiencing a special revelation. It's a matter of praying about it, keeping in touch with God, and then doing what seems to be the most reasonable thing. If there's something wrong with what you're doing, you'll be shown; you'll definitely become aware of it. I try to let God guide me, not through a blinding light but through an understanding faith and listening."

An understanding of these three principles should be helpful to the Christian who wants to get his career off on the right foot. But they are just the first steps in learning to work a Christian life. Now we are ready to explore the complexities of the working world and learn how the Christian faith can transform the rat race into a desirable, rather than a distasteful, daily experience.

2
What Is Success?

Americans have traditionally defined success in terms of concrete achievements, such as money, power, and social prestige. What, after all, is a "successful" businessman, if not a wealthy one? Or a "successful" professor, if not a prestigious one?

But the Christian approach to career goals is radically different from the usual ideas of success. One of the best explanations I've heard of the distinction between the Christian and non-Christian attitudes toward success was offered by a Dallas insurance salesman, Joe Miller.

"Becoming a Christian has not brought less work to me," he said. "I'm working harder than I've ever worked before. But since becoming a Christian, my whole attitude toward work and everything else has become quite different. Before I became a Christian, life to me was a hodgepodge of daily tasks, with no central focus, no clear-cut philosophic view that a sound ethical system could be built on. I've done very little in business that I couldn't defend ethically. But I think my ethics were based on practical considerations. The biggest problem that the non-Christian businessman has is that there's no continuity of action. You wake up in the morning, and business is the most important thing in the world to you. You're really going to burn the world up—at least this was my attitude. Becoming a success was the main thing, making the Million Dollar Round Table, becoming a Chartered Life Underwriter."

The Million Dollar Round Table, which Joe achieved for nine straight years, requires the sale of a million dollars of certain types of life insurance, primarily ordinary life, during a twelve-month period. The Chartered Life Underwriter (C.L.U.) certification involves several years of advanced study in business subjects.

"Business for a long time meant making more and more money and spending more and trying to have fun," he continued. "Trying to impress people we really didn't like. I justified this for a while by saying that I thought it was necessary for business. Now, I think that's wrong. I think it's much easier to do business with people when you present yourself as you truly are. Now, I really have some continuity, some singleness of purpose, some direction in my lifestyle. I don't have the feeling of traveling short distances in different directions each day. I know I'm going straighter, though I can't always see the ultimate destination God has in mind for me."

Joe also said his faith has completely reoriented his value system, altered his view of what is ultimately important and what is not in life. "Money has lost a lot of its appeal. I don't feel the same way that I did about finances a few years ago. I don't need the same financial position and income now. And my relationship to my family has changed so much. I would much prefer spending extra time with them now."

Another basic change is that his faith has removed the "personal proof" anxieties from his business life. "It's no longer a battle at work, where I have to prove my manliness. The ego involvement, the game playing, the status, the money—it's all a part of making the businessman think that success is the key. But then if he ever tries to define success, he's in trouble. Have you ever won a trophy for a game? When you get it, it's all gone. It's useless. That, to me, was business success."

Joe said that Christianity does not encourage him to work less hard. It's just that now he doesn't work for the same reasons. "I recognize business now for what it is: I work to get money to live on, and I also work to have the experience, to expose myself as a Christian to other people. I don't mean I go around grabbing people on street corners. But my job provides an opportunity to meet people and to put myself in a position where the Lord can use me. The work itself is just another part of my life now. It's not disproportionate. My job is more a practical necessity than anything else. That ego involvement—that unnatural drive that kills men at an early age—is gone.

"I don't believe that getting up in the morning early and working hard kills us. We die because of anxiety. We always believe that there's something over there that we've got to have. And when we arrive over there and get it, we find we don't want it. And then someone else whispers in our ear, 'No, it's not here, it's over there.' And then, like fools, we run over there. I spent thirty years doing that. And I found that for thirty years I had literally lived my life to please other people. And I wish I could say I lived my life to please a person, because then my life would have had continuity. But it was to satisfy people.

"One guy would say, 'You should be in the Million Dollar

Round Table.' And so I'd work toward that goal for a while. And then someone else would whisper another goal in my ear, and I'd run over and concentrate on that. In a limited way, I felt much like Solomon did in Ecclesiastes: It was all soap bubbles, all vanity. I reached the point of ultimate frustration. It just seemed to me that all I did was get up in the morning and go to the bathroom and go to the office. Some days I'd laugh and some days I'd play cards or hunt all day.

"I think more than anything else it was successes in business that the Lord used to bring me to the point of having to find him. Before I was successful, I was running so hard to be successful that I had no time to think about anything else. There are degrees of success, and I don't mean to say that I had reached the pinnacle, but the insurance business was very good to me. My problem was that I had no central reference point, no absolute in life. It's a matter of waking up each morning and spinning a wheel and saying, 'Okay, this is what I want to be today,' or I just waited for somebody to tell me what to be.

"And so, subconsciously, I committed myself ethically to a different value system each day. It was just a matter of my not being able to formulate how I felt about different moral issues. I'm not saying I didn't try. I've read most of the major philosophers, all the way to Nietzsche. It was an interesting exercise, but it didn't provide a practical way of running my life."

Joe's experience shows that a firm Christian faith, which imposes a purpose and continuity on the daily job, does not preclude the traditional success goals of money, power, and prestige. Rather, it helps us to put these goals in proper perspective and removes the anxiety of achieving without eliminating the achievement itself.

But the drive to achieve traditional career goals is always threatening to usurp the supremacy of Christ, and so the Christian has to be constantly on the alert to combat intemperate ambition. When we see a competitor using devious, underhanded methods to get ahead, we may feel at a disadvantage unless we also resort to the same means. Of course, most Christians would not consider killing or robbing in an effort to stay at the head of the rat race. But most of our temptations are more subtle and require us only to cut a moral corner here and there.

There is a New Jersey real estate salesman named Larry, for example, who competes daily with people who misrepresent the qualities of the land they are trying to rent or sell. "I decided at the outset that I would never be a high-pressure salesman who lies about his product," he said. "I never misrepresent what I'm selling. For instance, if I'm trying to sell a shopping center, I first get all my information and put it together, including the leases and how solid they are. I itemize every expenditure that went into the land during the previous year. And I try to be sure I'm not misleading the buyer on anything, no matter how small. In my sales pitch I mention any fault in the product, any possible expenditures which might not be readily visible at the time of the sale."

Nor does Larry feel that his honesty has put him at a disadvantage with his competitors. "If you include everything in your description of the property, you may miss a sale, but I can't honestly say I ever did. Of course, many of my competitors don't play the game the way I do. Some sellers may omit something in an expense statement that ought to be there. For instance, there are two kinds of expense reports. One kind is prepared for the Internal Revenue Service and includes every expense the owner can think of to keep his income as low as possible. The other kind of expense report is prepared when you get ready to sell the property. You try to make your expenses as low as you can so your income will appear to be as high as feasible. The expenses that are included in a property evaluation are such things as maintenance and tax expenses. But many property salesmen will put in last year's taxes for a sale this year. Because property taxes often go up from one year to the next, these salesmen can make their expenses seem lower and their income higher. I don't believe in doing this sort of thing because it's a lie, it's not honest. And in the long run, being honest hasn't lost me any business."

Larry concluded that there are two basic reasons for "playing it straight" with a buyer: "First of all, you have to consider your reputation if you're ever going to deal with a buyer or his acquaintances again. That's a practical consideration that applies to any businessman, whether he's a Christian or not. But in the second place, even if the chances are that the guy will never find out about a misrepresentation, it's important to me as a Christian to be honest and straightforward with my fellow men. It's not a question of whether or not I'll get caught. I have to live with myself and with God."

But apart from the temptations that accompany ambition, there is an even more serious danger that success harbors for the Christian. In a penetrating observation on the implications of business achievement, Jim Clinch, an office manager from Dallas, said, "Some may think it's impossible to be both a Christian and a success in business, but that's not so. I believe the Lord may bless a Christian with financial success. But perhaps the greatest danger is for a Christian businessman to become too successful. Christianity presents a paradox here, I guess. The more firmly you're committed to God, the harder and more efficiently you are inclined to work. And the harder you work, the more likely you are to become successful. But then as you get successful, you tend to fall away from God because you don't think you need him. When you have earthly possessions, it's hard to stay close to God. You rely on yourself and your acquisitions, and the material things tend to take God's place. If this happens, God may take your achievements away from you, or at least prevent you from enjoying them fully."

Nor is Jim Clinch the first person to make such an observation about the dangers of material success. In somewhat different words, Jesus declared in Matthew 19:24, ". . . it is easier for a camel to go through the eye of a needle than for a rich man to enter the kingdom of God."

A sensitive Christian, then, will not be satisfied with just any kind of success. And if he achieves certain worldly benefits, he will always be on guard to insure that they stay in their proper place and that Christ remains uppermost, in the driver's seat.

3
Has Hard Work Gone Out of Style?

Many employers love the phrase "hard work" because it conjures up images of efficient employees who willingly churn out product after product and assignment after assignment. And as the effort goes out, the money comes in and executive bonuses skyrocket to undreamed-of heights.

But employees often take a somewhat different view. For them, the virtues of hard work may seem merely an employer-originated myth based on an outmoded glorification of the Protestant ethic or the Horatio Alger hero. Hard work, in other words, is going out of style with an increasing number of workers because they cannot see any reason for it. Their jobs, often humdrum and devoid of social purpose, don't appear to warrant any special individual effort. Why tire yourself out so that you can't enjoy bowling with the fellows in the evening or relaxing with the family on weekends?

Instead of diligence, the ideal for many disillusioned employees is to become a boondoggle expert: a clever rogue who can get paid for eight hours work when he only puts in four; or the sly fellow who can manage to use up all his allotted "sick days" each year; or the woman who always has a perfect excuse when she arrives at work an hour late. The Goldbrick Age may indeed be upon us already!

But there has never been a place in the Christian scheme of things for goldbricking. As the Apostle Paul put it in 2 Thessalonians 3:7,8;10-12, ". . . we were not idle when we were with you, we did not eat any one's bread without paying, but with toil and labor we worked night and day, that we might not burden any of you."

Nor did Paul stop with a description of his own approach to work. Instead, he laid down the law for the lazy members of the Christian community at Thessalonica: "For even when we were with you, we gave you this command: If any one will not work, let him not eat. For we hear that some of you are living in idleness, mere busybodies, not doing any work. Now such persons we command and exhort in the Lord Jesus Christ to do their work in quietness and to earn their own living."

The apostle practiced what he preached, not only in Thessalonica but in the other Christian communities as well. Luke said in Acts 18:1-4 that Paul made it a point to stay with Priscilla and Aquila in Corinth because they were tentmakers. Their common trade provided him with an opportunity to earn his keep during the week so that he could preach about Christ every Sabbath. Every time I begin to feel sorry for myself because I have to drag myself out of bed and go to work, I usually can regain some perspective when I reflect on Paul's diligent example.

But why should a modern Christian feel a responsibility to work hard? Are Paul's principles still applicable to us? Without exception, the Christians to whom I spoke believed they had a duty to work diligently at their daily tasks.

"I think I have a responsibility as a Christian to do a good job, though not necessarily to be a success," declared

Vester T. Hughes, Jr., a leading tax attorney from Dallas. "The Christian faith requires you to give yourself to what has to be done. It's up to God how it comes out. I have probably worked too hard, but if the choice is between that and not working hard enough, I would choose working too hard. I don't think success *per se* is motivating me so much as the general feeling that I should do the best I can with whatever is at hand. I've told a number of younger lawyers that they have lost as human beings on the day their standard becomes someone who is not working as hard as they are but who is better paid."

One New York City government employee said, "I try never to complain about work that is given to me. I think when you're told by your employer to do a particular thing, you shouldn't say it's beneath you or that you feel you're getting too much work and the guy next to you is getting too little.

"Or if your boss asks, 'Would someone do this or that?' then the Christian should often be willing to volunteer. He shouldn't try to get away with the least amount of work. Rather than trying to see how little he can do and still get paid, the Christian should show he's not that kind of person. He should do that extra thing—go the extra mile, to paraphrase the words of Jesus' Sermon on the Mount—and show he's willing to make an additional effort."

But following this hard work philosophy is not always as easy in practice as it is in theory. Workers in some jobs have developed the art of boondoggling, or goofing off, to a near science, and if the Christian finds himself in such an environment, he may discover that he has to rub against the office grain.

"Many people in my office are goof-offs," an Atlanta secretary told me. "As a Christian I feel a responsibility not to waste time because I'm being paid to be faithful in my hours and my attendance. I feel in these matters that a Christian should set an example in working hard and not take time from the company that shouldn't be taken. That includes stretching coffee breaks, taking lengthy lunches, arriving late in the morning, chatting with other workers on company time. Our company is very lenient in these matters, and a couple of the girls have taken advantage of the situation.

"For the company's sake, I resent this laziness. I don't think it's right, because we're paid to do a certain job. When there is no work to be done, or the work is slack, our employers don't care if you take a long lunch break or some extra time at Christmas to do some shopping. They have been wonderful about this. But when we are pressured with work, then I don't think it's right, morally speaking, for anyone to goof off."

Carrying this idea of being a Christian example one step further, a Houston businessman criticized the custom in many companies of calling in sick to get an extra day off. "There's a lot of unnecessary absenteeism these days, a lack of conscientiousness on the part of many employees in my company," he said. "Mondays and Fridays are especially bad because people want to get long weekends. There may be a 10 percent absentee rate in our packing department on those days. They say you should never buy a car that was made on either of those days because of the number of auto workers that are usually absent. And if my company is any indication of what goes on in other industries, I believe it.

"I myself wouldn't call in sick if I weren't sick. I think a person should work the time the job calls for. There's a growing tendency for people to see how much they can get by with. But if a person's a Christian, he won't do this. Christianity teaches you have an obligation not only to God but also to your fellow man. I believe that the Lord wants you to give a day's work if you're paid for a day's work. Otherwise, you're stealing time from your boss. It's not being true; it's cheating your employer in the same way that taking money from his safe is cheating him. But a majority of the people I work with don't care; they don't see it as cheating."

On paper, these words may make sense. But actually living by them in a company where boondoggling customs have become deeply ingrained is another matter. It's much easier to do what everyone else is doing rather than what you know is right. Most of us tend to rationalize and compromise when we find ourselves in a situation where most of our co-workers—many of whom are also our personal friends—participate in a practice we know to be wrong. This conflict between our personal ethics and the customs followed by our occupational peer group is a recurrent theme not only on the hard work issue but also in many of the other topics we'll examine later in this book.

In a large corporation or government office, a little wasted time here and there may not have a discernible impact from the viewpoint of the individual employee. The effect becomes obvious usually on a cumulative basis, as the employer looks at the total work product of all his subordinates. But in some jobs, the results of a lack of diligence can be seen clearly and immediately by the individual worker. One poignant example is that of the lazy physician who has a careless attitude toward his patients.

A Philadelphia internist told me about how he combated such attitudes in a government-sponsored clinic where he worked. "The staff here has never developed an ethical standard by which it can measure its work," he explained. "Most of the doctors and administrators don't care that much about accomplishing anything. They're all standing around bickering and looking after their own self-interests. They're not willing to deny themselves when necessary.

"For example, when I first arrived, other doctors kept running into my office and saying how they were going to die or faint if they didn't go to lunch. As a Christian, I thought this was inconceivable when we had ten or fifteen patients waiting to be examined. My job is to see the patients, and I'm going to see them. If I get my lunch, fine. But my patients come first. If I have to give up something, such as my lunch, I'll do it. Or I'll come in early and work a little bit harder to make some order out of this mess. When you find yourself in a corrupt environment like this one, you have an ethical responsibility to do something to correct it. You either have to speak to somebody else about the bad attitudes, or help the administrator to organize the clinic better, or work harder yourself and perhaps deny yourself in some way."

This doctor, in the tradition of other committed Christians, decided to go against the office grain and challenge the corrupt customs of sloth and inefficiency. And he could see some improvement in his own work product, which was the treatment he gave to individual patients. But how about the organization as a whole and the other doctors who cared more for their own lazy habits than for the welfare of their clients? What are the prospects for one man being able to alter the entire environment?

"I think the main problem with the other workers here—and it's probably the main problem in most inefficient offices—is that they have no grass-roots leader," he explained. "There's no one to guide them. I'm working toward that kind of leadership in my little area. I'm saying that none of the existing attitudes and behavior standards are good enough for me. I think it's a cop-out. I'm starting a new standard, a Christian standard. But in the process of doing this, I'm not destroying the authority that exists, the power structure. I don't want to be the boss or the administrator. I just want to make it easier for the administrator. The constant bickering and laziness are not solving anything. What I'm trying to do is almost like a revolution, but an orderly and peaceful one. When it's accomplished, it doesn't mean that I'm the leader. But hopefully some order will emerge from this chaos."

One problem that this doctor is facing is that, by opposing clinic custom and making his opposition known, he has polarized the clinic's workers so that most are either for or against him. "They think I'm a new authority to contend with," he said. "They don't necessarily see the Christian ethic, even though that's what underlies my actions. I'm working hard to develop a broader concern for the sick people we're supposed to help, but to some of my coworkers that looks as though I'm a politician, that I'm wresting control from others for my own benefit. They don't realize that I'm only interested in eliminating all the confusion and that I'm ready to give any power I get back to them."

To correct the misunderstanding, he said, "I'm constantly

explaining to them what I'm doing. They don't always believe me, but I try. We have a legal mandate from the federal government that says we must help these indigent patients. My goal is for us to carry out that mandate and to fulfill the broader Christian responsibility to the sick and the needy. Although I haven't yet succeeded, except with respect to my own patients, it gives me a sense of satisfaction to know that I'm making some progress, making some people think in such extreme, difficult circumstances."

Nor does the Christian imperative to work hard and efficiently apply only to subordinate workers in an organization. The Christian boss also has a responsibility to be diligent, and if he shirks this duty, the result may be much more far-reaching and catastrophic than the sloth of the individual employee.

Justice Edward Thompson, administrative judge of the Civil Court of New York City, is an active Lutheran layman who believes wholeheartedly that hard work and efficiency are essential if justice is to be done in the courtroom. After serving as the city's fire commissioner and also as a trial judge in the state's Supreme Court and in various other city courts, Thompson was appointed administrative judge of the Civil Court in January, 1970.

When he took over, the Civil Court, which has jurisdiction over all civil claims of ten thousand dollars or less in the city, was plagued by a burgeoning backlog of nearly 137,-000 pending cases. Just two years later, the official annual court report showed that Thompson's 120 judges had disposed of about 317,000 cases—or 109,000 of the backlogged cases and 208,000 new matters.

Before Thompson assumed office, the plaintiff who

wanted to collect damages because of an auto accident or other personal injury typically had to wait a scandalously long time for a jury trial. It took from one year in Staten Island to more than four years in Brooklyn just for a case to be listed on the trial calendar. Thousands of cases lay idle for years thereafter before the trials actually began. After two years of Justice Thompson's supervision, the maximum trial delays were reduced to only one or two months throughout the city.

As a result of this progress, the January, 1972, Civil Court report marked the "first time since World War II" that the Civil Court calendar had been up-to-date. Thompson, in other words, had transformed one of the most inefficient and probably the busiest court system in the world into "the brightest star in the judicial firmament on dispositions," to use the words of retired U.S. Supreme Court Associate Justice Tom C. Clark.

Is there anything distinctive about Thompson's Christian convictions that has motivated him to apply his managerial talents so effectively to the troubled New York court system?

"I have always been impressed by the example of Saint Paul," he said. "He had power and riches and material things, but when he saw the light he gave it all up to work hard in spreading the gospel. He led a life of deprivation, was shipwrecked, languished in prison, and was eventually executed. But at all times he persevered and he believed. He is a tremendous example of what happens when you dedicate yourself to work hard and effectively. He had a full life, even though he possessed very little in the way of material things.

"One of my own motives for working hard is that I do care very much for my fellow man. The court is here because it belongs to the people. The court does not belong to the judges, the lawyers, the politicians. It belongs to the people. The people come into this court and they seek their remedies *now*. I believe there must be a day of reckoning in the court system, but when I first came here I found a morass of unfinished cases and lost files. It's totally irreverent, unmindful of the needs of the common man, to have a court run in that fashion. A court should stand for justice. There should be a validity of documents. I found that justice was being delayed and that the truth couldn't be found because you couldn't locate many papers and those you did find were often invalid because of sloppy procedures.

"This offended my sense of propriety and morality, and so I decided to do what I could do to change it. When I went out to talk to my judges and clerks, I found that they had similar desires. But in some way they lacked the leadership and the sense of direction to accomplish a better court system."

Court statistics clearly show that Thompson succeeded in transforming a horrible court system into a national model. He organized his judges into three-man teams—called the "conference and assignment system"—with one judge settling as many cases as he could and the other two team members trying the remaining matters without delay. But I wondered whether this efficiency, which was obviously beneficial to most litigants who used the courts, might be turning Thompson's subordinate judges and clerks into overworked human machines.

Thompson's answer was an emphatic *no*. He explained,

"One of the most important parts of a smooth-running operation is that anyone in the system can come in through an open door and complain or comment freely. My door's always open, the phone's always available. I go out of my way, possibly more than my predecessors, to visit each court. I visit each court at least once a month to see that things are running properly. It's too easy to sit in a chair behind a big desk like I have here and wait for things to happen, wait for trouble to begin. My philosophy is to visit people so that they know me and I know them."

Several of Thompson's clerks and judges confided that he is indeed a hard taskmaster. He has little patience with subordinates who show up late for appointments or who fail to do their jobs properly. But these qualities have not resulted in an impersonal working environment. Instead, the Civil Court staff members seem to have become fused into a more effective, spirited group than they were in the past. And they have, for the most part, returned the administrative judge's dedication to the court with a strong personal loyalty which can only bode well for the state of the judiciary in New York City.

But as the Christian works hard and tries to do his best, the potential for conflict with fellow workers becomes more apparent. Many people who prefer to slide along, doing a halfway job, know that the presence of a "hard charger," a co-worker who believes in diligence and striving toward excellence, can only make their own meager performances look bad in comparison. Ambitious non-Christian workers, on the other hand, may also take a dislike to the hard-working Christian because he represents a personal threat to them in their drive for promotions and raises. The Christian

worker, then, must be sure that his faith is firm and that his
communication with God is constant if he hopes to ride the
rough seas of conflict to the calmer waters of harmony with
co-workers.

4
Frustrations With Fellow Workers

If you ask the president of a corporation to describe his organization, he might say, "Oh, we're like a big family. We have our problems, but I think we basically get along pretty well together." Or maybe he would reply, "We're a team, all working together to make touchdowns on this big playing field of American industry."

But then if you move down to the rank-and-file accountant or secretary or clerk, the imagery becomes less highflown and probably more accurate: "This sweatshop? It's like a battlefield. Sure, there are some nice people here, but we've got our share of backstabbers, ambitious cutthroats, and just plain obnoxious jerks."

Christians who work in such a battlefield frequently find themselves being pulled in opposite directions by equally valid moral imperatives: First of all, they are committed to serving and loving their fellow workers. But they may find, in dealing with selfish or thoughtless co-workers, that this commitment sometimes clashes with their desire to develop their own abilities or with their responsibilities to their employers.

A helpful first step in learning to resolve this ethical dilemma involves an understanding of what Dr. J. William Worden, a Boston psychologist, has called "creative conflict."

"Christians generally extol peace and harmony, but I think the idea of peace at any price is bad for human relationships," he explained. "Creative conflict is an area we should explore further, because such conflict can bring growth in personal interactions. This could mean confronting an employee who is not doing a good job so that he can improve his performance. Or where two people are working closely together, it could mean getting latent hostilities out into the open so that mutual problems can be discussed frankly. If you postpone confrontations—whether at work, or in a marriage, or wherever—it may soon be too late to resolve the difficulties."

Time and again in my own job experience I've wrestled with the difficulty of maintaining a harmonious relationship with a fellow worker and yet at the same time trying to uphold my own integrity. One incident that sticks in my mind involved a fellow newspaper reporter who was assigned to cover a student demonstration with me. There were two story possibilities that developed after we arrived at the protest—a main article on the violence that had occurred, and a sidebar feature on what the students themselves thought about the incident. Our editors had not assigned us specific roles in reporting the event because no one had known at first what might happen. Since the other reporter had been on the paper longer than I and had specialized in events like this, he felt that he was entitled to write the main story.

But I bridled at his suggestion that I be relegated to the sidebar because I had been the first assigned to the story. Besides, he had arrived at the scene nearly an hour after I got there. I was also concerned that, if I gave in to him, I might be establishing a bad precedent: I might acquire the reputation of being a person who was easy to push around, or who did not particularly care whether he got a good assignment or not.

A heated argument ensued, and soon we were no longer on speaking terms. The office finally assigned him to the main story, and I got the sidebar. Ironically, the editors back in the office eventually merged the two stories and gave us both by-lines on the article.

I tried to repair my ruptured relationship with the other reporter in the next few days, but he had categorized me as an ambitious by-line hound and showed little interest in cultivating a friendship. Finally, because it was so uncomfortable to have an enemy in such close working quarters, I got desperate and did what I should have done in the first place: I prayed, asking God to straighten out the relationship. It worked. Within a day or two, we were exchanging "hellos"; we had an amiable conversation within a week; and we ate lunch together before the month was out.

A non-Christian might say, "Well, that problem would have worked itself out anyhow," but I don't believe it. Communication with God on the job—remembering that God has called me to be a Christian at work—has helped in too many situations for me to attribute the improvement in that relationship to anything but God's action. He works in my working life as effectively as he does at any other time if I remember to commit my problems to him.

But conflict with co-workers is not limited to competitive situations like the one I experienced. Sometimes the Christian worker finds himself dealing with a co-worker who is not vying for promotions or raises but is just naturally uncooperative. A Christian named Mike, who was an academic administrator at a large western university, faced just this problem.

"I've been having some problems with a man who runs the computer operation for our university," Mike explained. "This man—his name is Sam—typically refuses to reason with you once he's made up his mind, even though he may know he's wrong. The computer department does all the accounting for the school, but this guy has in essence said to me and others, 'I don't work for you, the client offices, but rather, you work for me.' And he tells us that if he decides to do something in a certain way, we're going to have to live with it."

Mike said that Sam would not take any suggestions and would not acknowledge that certain things had to be done by certain deadlines over which his computer department had no control. Paycheck processing was one example. One of the most serious disagreements the two men had was over whether a certain set of paychecks from Mike's department was going to be issued on time or several days late.

"I'm in charge of the computer end of issuing paychecks, and I'll decide when they come out," Sam stated flatly when Mike brought the problem to his attention.

"I can't subscribe to what you're saying," Mike replied. "Your job is important and critical, but you can't do it without the cooperation of the people who supply you with the data. If you don't move a little in our direction and try to cooperate with us, it seems to me that we'll have no alternative but to recommend to the administration that someone else should do your job."

"Are you trying to threaten me?" Sam retorted.

"It's not a threat. Just an attempt to be realistic. We get our information to you on time, and I think you should help us by getting our paychecks out on time. My people have bills to pay just like everyone else."

"Look, I'm handling my department in the way that the top university management wants me to," Sam replied. "I've talked with Dean Brown, and he agrees with what I'm doing."

Dean Brown, who was superior to both Mike and Sam, possessed "no computer background," Mike explained. And Sam had done a snow job in describing the paycheck problem to him by emphasizing only the computer department's viewpoint.

"I suspect we're never going to convince Sam," Mike said. "It won't be hard to show Dean Brown that the wool has been pulled over his eyes, and the impression I get from people I know at the top of the university administration is that Sam will eventually be moved to another job in the organization. I've had several conversations with the university president about this issue, but I really don't feel like I'm cutting Sam down behind his back. I've told him to his face what I think, and I feel that I have a broader responsibility to the organization. I've been honest enough to go to him and say, 'Hey, I don't think you're doing the right thing.' You have to balance off the well-being of everyone against the well-being of one individual. On the other hand, you have some responsibilities to that single man who is fouling up as an individual. But in trying to discuss the issue with a guy like Sam, it's hard not to end up making him mad.

"I've found that the people I work with can be categorized generally into three groups. First, there are the people who are genuinely responsive to suggestions. If they disagree, they'll discuss their position with you rationally. Secondly, there are those who appear to be responsive, but when you check back with them later, you find they were either not listening to you, or they were agreeing with you just to get you out of their hair. The third group includes people who are going to get angry at your suggestions, no matter how you approach them. They say, in effect, 'I'm going to do things my way, and I don't want to hear any of your suggestions.'

"Sam fell into this last group. But the important thing for a Christian who deals with people in any of these groups is to establish a sort of love relationship. If they get mad at you, it may be a matter of your saying, 'All right, so you got mad at me. But we both work here at the same place, and we'll continue to work here, hopefully. And so we've got to learn to work together. There are a lot of other people involved besides just the two of us. Now, how do we work ourselves out of this mess?'

"The way to show love sometimes is to keep the pressure on an unreasonable co-worker until the issue is presented in such a way that it has to be resolved. That's what I've been trying to do with this computer problem."

Conflicts with fellow workers, then, are inevitable in most job environments. And the Christian will frequently find himself having to carve a path between a variety of countervailing Christian moral principles. Creative conflict occurs when we strike a proper balance between at least three such principles: realizing our own human potential, showing love to individual fellow workers, and acting for the good of the entire organization.

I believe God expects Christians to take all three of these factors into account before we decide on a particular course of action. And the way to find God's will before we act always involves the same procedures: prayer, consultations with fellow Christians, study of the Scriptures, and a conscientious rational analysis of the situation. As the Christian follows God's will, he will become engaged in creative, rather than frustrating, conflict which can enhance relationships not only with co-workers, but also with subordinates and bosses.

5
How to Be a Human Boss

The boss of any organization is a peculiar creature. Most workers would agree in theory that he is a human being, but in practice they regard him as a kind of impersonal thing. Gossiping about the boss is almost the same as talking about the president of the United States, for the supervisor is a public figure who is not really "one of the guys." He gets paid more, he occupies a higher social status, and he wields more power than the ordinary employee.

The gulf between a superior and his subordinates has certain practical advantages for the employer and may be necessary, to some degree, to insure an efficient office. There is a tradition in the military that officers should not fraternize with enlisted men because it might endanger their ability to command, control, and gain respect. On the same theory, corporation executives often try to keep a social distance between themselves and their employees because they believe that excessive familiarity between supervisors and subordinates makes it more difficult to be fair and even-handed. An ability to discipline wayward subordinates and the freedom to reward deserving employees without incurring the charge of playing favorites depends upon maintaining a degree of impersonal detachment.

The old saying, "Familiarity breeds contempt," applies to

the Christian boss as well as the non-Christian. But there is a danger that the impersonal aspects of a job may become too prominent. It is at this point that the Christian faith has a great deal to say to those in the upper reaches of the corporate hierarchy. The temptation is sometimes overwhelming for a supervisor to overlook the humanity of his workers, for he may become obsessed with the quality and quantity of the work product or with the state of efficiency graphs. If this happens to the Christian boss, he is not only in danger of losing his capacity to love, but he is also likely to create a disgruntled work force that may sabotage company operations out of spite.

The challenge of balancing these personal and impersonal tendencies is reflected in an experience of Mark, a district sales manager for a large machinery company in the Midwest. He faced a particularly uncomfortable situation when he learned that one of his traveling salesmen, Silas, had become a problem drinker. Silas and Mark had started working in the company at the same time, and they saw a great deal of each other until Mark was promoted.

"I learned that he resented the fact that I'd been promoted and he hadn't," Mark told me. "He didn't act jealous around me, but he told some secretaries in the office that he didn't see how I had been promoted instead of him."

Mark first became aware of the drinking problem when he, Silas, and some of the other salesmen were returning on a train from a convention in Chicago. Silas stayed drunk during most of the journey, but Mark didn't warn him because they were not involved in any selling on the trip. But the manager did begin to check his subordinate's work more closely after that, and he learned Silas was doing some heavy drinking even when he met customers.

"He was drinking in the morning, and he was drinking in the afternoon," Mark said. "I'd call him in the morning when he should have been on the road, but he'd still be in the hotel. And you could tell he had been drinking from the way he talked. Also, sometimes he'd call into the office, and the secretary who answered the phone would realize something was wrong, because he'd be slurring his words or not talking coherently.

"Then, it got to the point where I had to check with some of his customers. You have to check, just to make sure. I warned him two or three times and put him on probation, and he promised faithfully he would quit. His customers, even though they were his friends, finally would admit that he was drunk when he came in to see them. It affected the way he was doing his job. When a person comes in to make a sales visit during the day and he's intoxicated, the customers don't have much respect for him. And that also means they don't have much respect for your products or your company."

Mark finally decided that the end had come. He made an appointment to talk at Silas's home and met him there in the presence of his wife.

"We've discussed this situation many times before," Mark began. "You've been on probation, and you've repeatedly failed to live up to your promise to quit drinking. You've demonstrated you can't drink moderately, that you can't wait to do your drinking after working hours. We're going to have to do what we said we'd do if you didn't take care of this. We'll have to relieve you of your position, and I've come down here to check you out and to pick up your car."

Silas didn't plead because he seemed to know what was coming. He only said, "I think you're wrong, but if that's the way it is, okay."

But his wife was more hostile. "You don't know what you're talking about," she shouted through a flood of tears. "You've always been afraid of Si, that he might take your job away from you. He doesn't drink that much, and you know it!"

She continued to abuse Mark for several more seconds, but he departed without replying to her charges.

Firing a worker under these circumstances presents a touchy situation because the man doing the firing is always vulnerable to the charge that he was mainly interested in eliminating a potential rival. But Mark was convinced he had handled the problem as well as he could under the circumstances. He had prayed at every step. He had warned Silas and given him several chances to rehabilitate himself. Then, when the well-being of the company and its customers came into jeopardy, he had decided he had no choice except to tell Silas to leave.

But perhaps even more difficult than firing a potential competitor is the problem of firing a close friend.

"I had worked with Tim for years—he was a wholesale distributor's representative and I was his immediate supervisor—and we were always close friends," declared one Oklahoma businessman. "I first noticed he had been drinking too much when he was driving a vice-president and me from the home office down to his office one day. I was in the back seat and this vice-president was in the front, next to Tim. The car began to ease off the side of the highway, and Tim jerked it back a couple of times. The third time, the man in front looked back at me, and so I said, "Tim, you

want me to drive?'' He said, 'Yeah, I don't care if you do.'
He got in the back seat and immediately fell asleep.

"I got to checking up on him and found he was drinking
vodka in the morning pretty often. At sales meetings or
conventions, he'd disappear about 5 P.M. He'd just go to his
room and start to drink. I had talked to him several times and
said, 'You're going to have to quit this.' I had gone with him
to his doctor, and the doctor said he'd been prescribing
tranquilizers for his blood pressure. Apparently, the alcohol
and the pills had a double effect and made him sleepy all
the time.

"One time, I did something I never felt quite right about.
We had a meeting in Houston, and it was supposed to start
at 8:30 in the evening. This old boy, Tim, didn't show up,
and so I went to his room. I saw he had a bottle of liquor.
He was out cold. I went back to the meeting, but I didn't
tell the other people he was drunk. I said he was sick, which
was the truth, in my opinion. Then some of my superiors
expressed concern about his condition and said they were
going to go down to see him. I ran down to his room ahead
of them and hid the bottle of liquor. I was possibly wrong
to do that. But I've always tried to inspire the feeling in the
people I'm associated with that they can count on me. And
I don't set myself up above them because of their bad
habits, because I know I do things that are wrong, too. But
in protecting your employees, you have to decide whether
you're being dishonest or untruthful. I still had hope for this
guy, and I knew if these executives had found him drunk,
he'd probably have been fired on the spot.

"That hidden bottle saved him temporarily, and for a year
or two after that the guy seemed to be doing his job all right.

But then his work began to slip. The sales went down, and we checked with some of his customers and they admitted he was often drunk on the job. He was in danger of losing some big accounts, too. So finally, when the situation seemed to be impossible, I had to let him go.

"I suppose, in the long run, that all I did by hiding that bottle was to prolong what had to happen. But we had worked together for such a long time and were such good friends that I wanted him to have every chance."

This Christian businessman, by his own admission, may have allowed the personal side of his supervisory function to get out of hand. Several Christians I spoke to said that they try to avoid hiring friends for that very reason—that it's too hard to be firm, to discipline a friend in the same way you might sanction the improper actions of a casual acquaintance.

But firing is not the only area in which a Christian boss must weigh the personal and the impersonal features of his job. Suppose a secretary comes to you with a personal problem and asks your advice? Should you agree to help her on company time; or should you tell her you can only talk to her at the end of the day; or should you refuse to discuss her personal problems altogether?

Jim Bruce, an associate dean of engineering and a housemaster at the Massachusetts Institute of Technology, said that he maintains an open-door policy for his students and other subordinates. "If a student comes by to see me, I'm going to find time to see him then, rather than making an appointment three or four days later," he said. "I think this is a way of expressing Christian love. The Bible tells us to bear one another's burdens. As Christians today we tend to live our own tightly compartmentalized lives, not sharing ourselves with other people. Devoting so much time to students with their individual problems can cut down on the efficiency of my own work some days. But I think personal relationships have to take precedence, even though administrative efficiency is certainly important."

Most of the Christians I talked to felt it was important to devote some time to advising troubled employees about their personal problems. But a common warning was that the boss has to be careful not to allow himself to become too much of a counselor.

"Many employees will take advantage of a boss's good nature if he develops the reputation of having an ear for any personal problem," one Christian businessman said. "You can become a crutch for people like that and end up hurting them more than you help. I try to be discriminating. If a secretary or clerk keeps coming back to me with the same marriage problem, I let them know in a nice way that I've helped them as much as I can in light of my position. I let them know that there are just so many hours in the day and that I can't really do their problem justice anymore. Then, I suggest that they seek advice from a professional—a marriage counselor or minister or psychologist. After all, some of us are called to such jobs, according to the way I read Paul's Epistles. And I'm going to foul up everything if I try to usurp everyone else's function."

Jim Rains, a Dallas real estate dealer, summarized the role of the Christian employer this way: "In a supervisory position, you're in a position of trust with the company. You have to look after the company's interests as well as the individual's. You advise and warn your subordinates up to a point, and then beyond that point, you have to give the company's interests priority. As a Christian supervisor, you have to work with the person first. If that doesn't work out, then your Christian responsibility to the company takes over.

"I think that, whatever your management position, if you don't try to perform to the best of your ability on the job, you ought not to be there. There's a responsibility to work hard yourself and to see that those under you do the same. Otherwise, a supervisor may in effect be stealing time from the company, or allowing another to steal the company's time, and that's not right. If you're over a person, you have to be sure he's not goldbricking. If you allow somebody to get away with that, in the long run it's going to hurt everybody in the company. It could mean salaries will be lowered and business will lag. And it hurts the morale of the other workers who are trying to do their jobs."

Although Christian employers may be concerned about trying to balance individual and organizational considerations, many other supervisors fail to consider the human issues at all. When Christian workers find themselves working under impersonal, even "beastly" bosses, their patience and faith in God's ability to act may be strained to the breaking point.

6
Handling a Beastly Boss

A young woman came home from her job one day on the verge of tears. "I hate that man, I absolutely detest him! He's a total creep!"

"Who?" her husband asked, well knowing the monster to whom she referred.

"My boss, Mr. Jenkins, that's who!"

"So what happened today?"

"He refused to give me a raise, he bawled me out for not finishing one of my two million reports on time and then he shut the door in my face when I tried to explain why the report was late. What can a person in my position do?"

After thinking for a moment or two, her husband shrugged and replied, "I guess you can quit."

And sometimes resignation from the company is often the first thing that pops into the mind of the worker who finds himself butting heads with an obnoxious boss. Dealing effectively with a competitive or hostile co-worker is unpleasant enough. But in that situation the employee is still on an equal footing with his adversary and has some room to maneuver in trying to get along with him. The supervisor, on the other hand, operates by definition on a higher power level, and so the worker's range of response is more limited.

Some workers, fearing they are bound to lose in any

direct confrontation with a bad boss, may resort to sabotage, boondoggling, or petty pilfering. But such frustrated efforts to get back at an employer, to even things up, are not part of the Christian's arsenal of legitimate offensive weapons. He plays by a different set of rules and in the long run probably has a better chance of improving his working environment than those who resort to more devious means.

Bill, the chief accountant in a Philadelphia company, described one way a Christian might conduct himself with a difficult supervisor: "The office manager in our company used to be a guy who worked on nervous energy, and he and I were always at odds on office procedures. If there were two ways of doing something, he'd do it one way and I'd do it another. It made things a little difficult at times, and we had some little clashes.

"For example, if he wanted something done in a hurry, he'd stand over an employee and watch. I'm one who will give it to an employee who I know is capable of doing a decent job, and then go back to my desk. We had one gal who was an excellent worker. She ran an accounting machine and showed a rare combination of accuracy and speed. He got on her so badly that she finally quit. He'd just stand over her and exude this tense and nervous attitude. He also operated on the theory, 'Never let a guy know he's doing a good job.' He would point out all the bad things. The first thing on Monday mornings, he handed out memos, and if you didn't get one, you could assume you were doing all right, I suppose, because they were always critical. The memos never praised you for the good things you might have done. Not getting one was a sort of compliment by omission.

"It doesn't make sense for me to operate like that, and I let him know it on occasion when he'd criticize a good employee. I'd try to do it subtly, saying that maybe it would be a good idea for *us* to give the efficient, responsible people more recognition in their operations. I'd always say 'us' or 'we' rather than accusing him by saying 'you,' but I think he got the point."

The two men remained at odds until the office manager was transferred to another city, but while they worked together, Bill succeeded in avoiding any outright confrontations or arguments. "There were never any harsh words between us. Since he was the boss, I did it his way, even though I tried to let him know where I stood. When he was on vacation and I was asked to fill in for him, I did it my way, but I wasn't one to push the point when he was there.

"I used to worry about it some because he got on my nerves as well as those of the other employees, but I found I could consistently get rid of my worries and anxieties by praying to God for help. I'm firmly convinced that when you turn these problems over to the Lord, you quit worrying about them. You do your best, the way you feel it should be done, and then you quit worrying about it. It's a matter of living by the principle in Psalms 37:5: 'Commit your way to the Lord, trust in him, and he will act.' If you turn problems over to the Lord, you'll definitely have less to worry about."

Sometimes, however, a Christian's relationship with a boss can get more explosive. One Christian woman, Martha, who ran an adult education program for a California community center, told me that her troubles began when a new director of the community center assumed office.

"I set up the entire program and did all the planning and all the publicity for the new semester before this director, Mr. Sanders, arrived," Martha said. "I wrote the news releases, met the important people in the news media, even did some public speaking. In the previous year, I had already done the hiring and chosen many of the courses. A lot of people who took the courses the first year thought it was a good program and had decided to come back for further instruction.

"But I guess I got off on the wrong foot with Mr. Sanders from the outset. He was obviously never comfortable with me, even though he was buddy-buddy with all the men who headed the other departments at the center. I was the only woman in a position of responsibility. When he was first made director, he said he wanted to take all his subordinate managers out to lunch. When my turn came, he said he wanted to know all about me. I did most of the talking, but he didn't seem all that interested. He appeared to want to get back to work. After this lunch, I found I always had to initiate conversations. It was embarrassing. He never even made an effort. He never once looked in on a class in my department and seemed to have no idea about who came to the program or who was teaching. I wondered why he never commented about what I was doing, but I just tried to be friendly with him."

Then one day before the new semester started, Mr. Sanders announced to Martha that he was going to discontinue the adult education program entirely and redirect the educational resources into other channels at the center. She said she reacted "mildly" at first.

"Look, Mr. Sanders, a lot of people have been counting

on this program," she said. "Isn't there a chance you might reconsider? We have a group of students here who have almost finished studying for their high-school equivalency exams. We really should give them a chance to complete their courses, don't you think?"

"No, I don't think that's sufficient cause in itself."

"But there are twelve teachers who have given up their summers to teach these courses," she replied, becoming more exasperated. "Their contracts are sitting in there on my desk waiting to be signed, and it's too late for them to make other plans."

"I'm sorry, Martha, but that's the way it is."

With that, the young woman hit the ceiling.

"You're doing an awful thing," she exploded. "You're not really interested in anything that's going on around here. You think you can just do as you please, snap your fingers and it will be done."

"Now Martha. . . ."

"Now nothing! Who do you think you are, God or somebody? You just snap your fingers and close a program even though you know so much work has gone into it and so many people are involved."

They sat quietly for a moment, and then Martha spoke. "Why couldn't we have discussed cutting the program down, streamlining it, trying to make more money from it?" she finally asked. "I've been thinking for some time I might like to do a little teaching at night, maybe have this as my night job. I think I could have managed this program part-time."

Mr. Sanders sighed. "That might have been an alternative, I suppose," he finally replied. "But I couldn't ask you to take over on that basis now, not after this."

Looking back on the incident, Martha told me, "I think he really wanted to consider that part-time idea, but there was no chance after the argument. I was angry, and I don't believe the approach I took was the right one. I said the wrong things, but the time had certainly come to say something. In the future, if I could foresee how a man like that might act, I would be more outgoing. I'd barge into his office, ask his opinion more often on different subjects, force him to communicate with me. That was our main problem—a lack of communication. He obviously was not as interested in establishing lines of communication as I was, and so I should have pushed him. But it's hard, when you're the subordinate, to force yourself on a boss. Yet sometimes it has to be done. You have to make the tough boss like and respect you not only by quietly doing a good job but also by being aggressive in establishing a personal relationship.

"But an experience like the one I had is still hard for a Christian to accept. After I left that job, the first thing I did was to go through all the spiritual things I'd been taught. I had prayed, but God still had not allowed me to keep that job. Then I remembered the verse in Romans 8:28, 'that in everything God works for good with those who love him, who are called according to his purpose.' I decided there had to be a reason behind this awful experience. Somehow there had to be some good coming out of it.

"Several months went by, but I couldn't get over being resentful. Finally, after I got another job and had more time to reflect, I decided that perhaps I had become too obsessed with that education program. To me, a job becomes a mission if I like it. I get so enthused that the job becomes my life. I was there day and night. I'm not sure that was entirely bad, but I do remember cutting corners in preparing for the Sunday-school class I was teaching. I wasn't regulating my life to leave time for everything that was important. And so maybe God was just letting me know that I had overdone it with that job, that I was getting carried away on my own steam and not relying on him enough."

But some workers are not content to let the final decision on an important work issue rest with an immediate superior. Occasionally, the conflict in viewpoints may be so fundamental and serious that the Christian may feel he should appeal to the "boss of bosses" in his organization. A public health official named Marvin said that he encountered this situation with a supervisor in a poverty health funding project.

"Everybody that wanted federal money from us had to submit an application and these applications could run anywhere from 10 to 250 pages long," Marvin explained. "I was supposed to review these documents and evaluate their impact on the communities involved. My supervisor, Mr. Parks, might give me 30 or more of these at a time, and I'd work very, very hard to turn them out. He'd say, 'They have to be done, they absolutely have to be done right away.' I handwrote or typed many of them myself to be sure I met his deadlines.

"The problem was that Mr. Parks would often lose these applications or just forward them on to the next office without reading them. Then, he'd come in some mornings fuming about some newspaper article which criticized a program that had been improperly funded. 'Didn't you give me a report on this?' he'd shout.

"I'd get a copy of my report, which I had forwarded to him weeks before and which as often as not recommended that the program be sacked, and I'd show it to him. Then he'd say he hadn't seen the report and walk off. It was all so bizarre. He was constantly abusive, even on the smallest matters. It was almost as though he wanted to destroy my ego. He'd take one of my reports, for example, and say sarcastically, 'Don't you know any better than this? Surely you're not this stupid.'

"He'd also demand to see things before they were finished and then criticize me for not doing a thorough job. Finally, I began to doubt myself. And so I started consulting other individuals, including many of my fellow workers. I found that Mr. Parks was having trouble with other people, too. I also learned that most of my work was being widely accepted by people who received it in other offices, even though it was consistently being criticized and sneered at by him."

Marvin emphasized that he gave his boss the benefit of every doubt before he tried other channels to remedy the problem. "I think that was a way of turning the other cheek, as Christ told us to do," he explained. "I tried to see how I might be learning something, both professionally and psychologically, from my exposure to Mr. Parks. I didn't lash out at him when he attacked me. Before I took any action against him, I looked at myself as objectively as possible in relation to his position in the office.

"But when it became obvious to me that he was acting unfairly, I became less willing to change. I challenged his evaluations of my work more often, but that seemed to have no effect. And as I say, it wasn't just my problem. The morale of the entire office had slipped perceptibly in the time that he had worked there. Finally, I went to see a man who was superior to both Parks and myself and explained the problem that I was facing. I told him that if things didn't change soon, I would have to leave. This man was very interested in having me stay in my job. I asked him to give me another job that would be more independent of Mr. Parks, and he said he'd see what he could do. But he told me that I might have to wait a few months because nothing was available at the time. I didn't feel that I could put up with the situation that long, and so I finally decided to leave.

"In going over my supervisor's head, I acted out of a sense of responsibility to myself, but I also wanted to see that justice was done to other people in the organization. But I think reporting a superior is a last resort. I would always try to work things out with the boss before taking such action. I exhausted every other possible remedy. It's an irrevocable step, to report a supervisor. It's sort of like university administrators' calling the police in to quell a student riot. Lines of communication are automatically severed. But in this situation I think I put up with the abuse longer than most people would have. You just have to weigh the risk to your own future against the concrete good you'll accomplish by going over your boss's head."

It takes considerable courage to report a bad boss to one of his own superiors. You may lose your job and you certainly can't expect a good recommendation for the next one. But there are even greater risks—up to and including the possibility of being blackballed by a group of prospective employers—when the worker decides to step entirely outside his organization and publicly blow the whistle on his employer's misdeeds. Some Christians, after considerable prayer and thought, have felt compelled to take this ultimate step to counter a supervisor whose acts seem grossly unjust or even immoral.

7
The Limits of Loyalty, or When to Blow the Whistle

Many Christians are as loyal to their companies as they are to God and country. They may disagree with some company policy, or they may occasionally become upset when they don't get a raise or a promotion. If job frustrations become unbearable, their ultimate act of defiance may be to resign in a huff.

But it's the rare employee who would consider reporting an employer to government authorities or to the press. Such "whistle blowing" smacks of the double cross, of playing the stool pigeon. And a stool pigeon, even if he informs on his buddies out of the loftiest, purest motives, is widely regarded as one of the lowest forms of human life in our society.

Christians, in blindly accepting this anti-informer mentality, may be denying one of the most powerful forces in their faith—the higher morality that transcends loyalty to any earthly organization. Because we so often have a vested interest in the established economic power structures, we assume that our superiors, though certainly not perfect men, are highly unlikely to do anything *really* wrong. And so we accept without question their moral standards, including the way they treat their employees and the quality of product they turn out for public consumption.

One businessman told me, "I think company loyalty is the top thing you have to consider in working on a job. It's not up to the employee to judge or criticize management. I've always second-guessed some of management's decisions, but at the same time I always said they didn't get to that position by being stupid. They usually come up with the right answers, and you have to respect them for that."

But to take an extreme example, what if you are a government employee and your superiors embark on a policy of ethnic extermination, as the Nazis did against the Jews in Germany? Or what if you work for an airplane manufacturer, and your boss instructs you to use defective parts that will endanger the safety of airline passengers? In either of these cases, the thoughtful Christian would have trouble living with himself unless he fought his employer's actions.

And the situations that pose a whistle-blowing issue range across a broad social and economic spectrum: Suppose your boss engages in systematic racial discrimination in his hiring practices—an obvious violation of the equal employment opportunity provisions of the 1964 Civil Rights Act? Or what if your company's executives are engaging in price-fixing with competing firms, thus driving up the price the public must pay for consumer goods?

Each of these examples raises serious questions for the Christian conscience. But, as Ralph Nader and other contributors point out in Nader's book, *Whistle Blowing*, there are many factors that a worker must consider before he steps outside his organization and goes to the public with his case.

First of all, the employee must decide whether the misbehavior of the employer is sufficiently serious and whether the evidence is strong enough to justify the risks of whistle blowing. For the informant will be in danger not only of losing his job, but also of being blackballed throughout his entire industry for his actions. And the worker should be sure of his facts: he must not rely on rumor or secondhand information as a basis for his accusations. The employer's reputation, as well as the economic security of the worker and his family, may be at stake in a whistle-blowing situation, and wild or questionable charges against the boss must be avoided. Finally, the worker who plans to report his boss should exhaust all channels of appeal within his organization before putting his case before outside authorities. In most cases, the employee's sole purpose is to make the employer alter some illegal or immoral practice, and if this goal can be achieved without public exposure, so much the better for all concerned.

A Christian named Tom, who was a teacher in a Texas high school, had an encounter with the administrators of his school system which illustrates many of the procedures and problems that the informing worker faces. "As I look back on it, the seeds of my problems in that school were sown during my first year of teaching," Tom said. "I was assigned to teach mathematics, but I occasionally talked about things that were happening on the national scene. For example, a student would come in and ask me if I was going to observe a national moratorium day to protest the Vietnam war. I'd make some comment that I thought we were wrong being in Vietnam, but that I didn't think anything was being accomplished by wearing an armband or joining a protest march. I felt that demonstrations were producing no results, and that trying to influence national leaders through other means might be more fruitful. These statements didn't get me into any direct trouble during the first year I taught there, however.

"But in the second year, I ran into some difficulties. I wasn't saying as much as I usually had on the Vietnam situation, but the fact that I was antiwar was known among all the students and teachers. And so I was invited to one history class to debate the war with an administrator from the school district. I seemed to have the administration's approval to express my views at that point."

Later that year, the students asked permission to change their dress code. The girls wanted to wear slacks on days when it was cold, and they had been prohibited from doing this in the past. And boys wanted to wear their hair longer than their shirt collars—the acceptable limit at that time in the school. There were some student council debates on what would be a suitable dress code from the students' point of view, and the students planned to present their recommendations to the principal and the school board for approval. Both faculty members and students were invited to come to one meeting, and Tom decided to attend at the suggestion of one of his students.

"There were so many kids who wanted to speak at the meeting that I didn't get a chance to say anything," he explained. "And so I thought I'd write something up and let them have it to read. I drafted a proposed code, and we passed it out. I planned to give a copy to the principal the next morning because I was going to ask permission from him to put this viewpoint into the teachers' mailboxes. I feel that issues such as this ought to be debated."

But the principal called Tom in before the teacher had a chance to explain his intentions. "Did you hand these sheets out to your classes?" the principal asked. "I found one of them on one of the student's desks."

"No, I didn't pass them out to my classes—only to the student council members at the request of the student council president," Tom replied.

"Well, don't do this again," the principal ordered.

At Tom's March evaluation, the principal said he was going to recommend that Tom be rehired on probation because there were several things he felt Tom should correct in his teaching. "He had never notified me that he planned to take this action, and I was taken by surprise," Tom said. "I felt a little bit picked on."

"You're a little too controversial, Tom," the principal explained at the evaluation meeting. "Anything you want to say to students in the future, which you know goes against the administration's viewpoint, has to be cleared with me first before you say anything."

"Well, just what is it I'm going to have to correct to be taken off probation?" Tom asked. "What specific kinds of things have you disagreed with? I didn't know you were aware of what I've been saying to my students."

"I'll write out my objections," the principal replied, and Tom received a list several days later.

"It was everything he could rake up on short notice," Tom told me. "One thing was that I should never speak to a student about the choice of a college. In particular, I had spoken to a student about going to a particular college, and had advised him against it. I had tried to counsel this student and was qualified to do so since I had a counseling certificate. But his parents got upset about what I said and complained to the principal.

"I was also accused of passing out controversial literature in classes—that was the dress-code proposal I drafted. I had already assured the principal I would not do that again before clearing it with him. And there were other little things: I was supposed to have improperly allowed students to eat in one of my classrooms during a drama club meeting that I was sponsoring. But those things weren't really bothering him. It was the fact that I had expressed myself on controversial matters and that he disagreed with my positions. I didn't just keep quiet about things."

After Tom had read the list of objections to his performance, he signed the teacher-evaluation report. But he told the principal he thought the charges against him were unfair and asked permission to write a rejoinder to the principal's criticisms. The principal consented and said he would put Tom's answer into the file with the other papers.

"I went down his objections point by point in my rejoinder," Tom said. "He charged I was getting to school late: I said there was no evidence of this. He said I improperly allowed kids to eat in my classroom: I pointed out that he had given his permission for this to be done during the drama club meetings. He had apparently forgotten about that. I wrote that I thought I had the right to advise people about where to go to college, but I agreed not to engage in this sort of consultation any more. He didn't specify the Vietnam issue, but he said that I should not be so controversial and should clear my viewpoints on different issues with the administration before I expressed them. I said that I didn't know the administration had a point of view that I had to clear my opinions with. I also said I didn't discuss many controversial topics, such as where I went to church or who I supported for president. I indicated that I did oppose crime, violence, drug abuse, and the war."

The principal, after receiving Tom's defense of his actions, decided to change his recommendation to the school board. Instead of recommending probation, he advised the board not to renew the teaching contract at all.

"In effect, he reacted to my talking back," Tom said. "He thought I should just say, 'Yes sir,' and then toe the line. My view was that his authority did not extend over me in matters of free speech. He didn't tell me before the board meeting that he had changed his recommendation, and so I didn't appear at the meeting to defend myself.

"When I heard that I wouldn't be hired again, I didn't know exactly what to do. I began to inquire around and was told by a friend that I should probably contact a lawyer. But I decided that, before I did that, I would exhaust all avenues of appeal within the school system itself. I think that's important because that way you avoid taking impulsive action. And also you're less likely to get involved in overkill by going for a remedy that is more serious than you actually need."

Tom said he went to his principal on three separate occasions after being notified of his nonrenewal.

"Is there any chance you might change your recommendation to the board so that I could get another contract?" he asked.

"I'm afraid not, Tom. That was a board decision and I can't change it now. But I'll write you an excellent recommendation. Besides, I really don't think you and I could get along if you stayed here. It's out of my hands now, and I just can't change it."

"Well, if you take that position, you're only leaving me the alternative of an appeal of some kind if I'm going to pursue this," Tom replied.

"If you appeal, remember you have a wife and children to support," the principal said. Tom took this remark to mean that he would not get a good recommendation if he did appeal.

After some thought and prayer, Tom decided to go to the school superintendent.

"I'm not going to change anything," the superintendent told him. "It could be that your principal made a mistake, but if I found out one of my teachers disagreed with me on anything, I would have gotten rid of him the first week."

Tom's next step was to seek advice from officials at his state teachers' association, and they advised him to go the legal route.

"I finally did decide to hire a lawyer and go to court, but it took a lot of thought and prayer and family consultations," Tom said. "I was advised by some friends, some other teachers, just to let the thing drop and get another teaching position in a nearby town. But there were some other local school officials who had heard about the problem, and my professional reputation had suffered. I wanted to correct that. I also felt that I should be put back in my old teaching job because I was the victim of an unjust nonrenewal. It was a prejudiced, arbitrary action, from my point of view. There was a prior censorship involved in what I had a right to say, and I felt that was a violation of my First Amendment rights to free speech. And there seemed to be an overall lack of due process: Under Texas law as a public employee I was supposed to be given an open, public hearing by the school board. But they had refused when I showed up at one of their meetings with my lawyer.

"I've long been committed to seeking justice in society, and I've always had a deep interest in applying Christian ethics to social problems. Our social system is based on principles of equality of treatment and reasonable freedom of expression, and I felt as though the treatment I had suffered was a violation of those principles. If it could happen to me, it could happen to anybody, and so I decided I should stand up and be counted and attempt to change society in an orderly, rather than a revolutionary, way. The courtroom seemed the best place to do this. I knew other teachers had confronted problems similar to mine. It would be uncomfortable for me and would require money from our family savings. I knew I might even ruin my professional reputation in the state and completely eliminate the possibility of being employed there. But I felt that no teacher should have to face such an arbitrary renewal policy, and I appeared to be in a stronger position than most. I had several advantages: A graduate degree from a good school; enough savings to hire a lawyer; and a wife who could go to work if need be. The strong members of a profession should be the ones who are willing to risk the most, especially if they are Christians. And so we took the risk."

Tom's specific Christian rationale for going to court was, "This is God's world and God acts through people and movements to make this a better place for everyone to live. God, I believe, wants justice in the world, where one powerful group cannot destroy those that are weaker. Christians, especially in a democratic system like ours, have a responsibility to oppose unjust institutions and laws and customs in order to secure a more just and moral society."

In terms reminiscent of the Apostle Paul in Colossians 3:14, he explained that one of his Christian assumptions is "that there should be harmonious relationships between people. Our working environment—in fact, all our institutions—should encourage these harmonious relationships so that love can be expressed. For genuine harmony to exist under our governmental system, there cannot be a repression of the freedom to express different viewpoints. Administrators should not have an absolute right to push their employees around just because they disagree with the employee's opinion on different issues.

"Besides, in my particular situation my teaching contract didn't provide for my being subject to the restrictions the principal tried to impose on me. There was nothing that said I had to keep my mouth shut about relatively harmless issues that came up with the kids. As a matter of fact, other teachers freely expressed their opinions on the very topics he was trying to make me stop discussing, but they took positions that coincided with the principal's own beliefs. What it all boiled down to was that I was being discriminated against."

And so Tom decided to challenge the propriety of the nonrenewal of his teaching contract in court. But even after becoming convinced of the justice of his cause, Tom still had some reservations about using a public lawsuit as a weapon to blow the whistle on his employer.

"In a way, I felt guilty about being in a suit where I was asking damages," he said. "That seemed almost non-Christian. Money wasn't my initial goal. What I wanted was to get my job back as fast as possible, but now I'm teaching outside the state, and so my original purpose has become almost academic, I suppose. I'd like to get back what I've spent to litigate this matter, of course, but my lawyer has asked for much more. I don't want people to think I'm just a greedy guy without other principles that I'm fighting for. But I suppose that imposing damages on the school system would be a form of discipline, a sanction for them. In other words, if you don't demand damages, a legal judgment against them would have no effect. I want them to think twice before they make another teacher go through this. As I say, I'm not entirely satisfied with the damage approach, but I guess it's the only form of discipline that's available to me."

As of this writing, there has been no final decision in the case, but that's not really the point of Tom's experience. The main lesson for us is that as Christians we must be open to the possibility that God may someday call us to blow the whistle to protect others from harm or injustice. Both the Apostles Peter and Paul taught that Christians should be subject to "every human institution," and for contemporary Americans that means upholding such rights as freedom of speech and due process of law. (See 1 Peter 2:13 and Romans 13:1.) If we are expected to be participating citizens under our governmental system and yet sit idly by when those rights and laws are being threatened, how can we say we're upholding our institutions? Tom faced an injustice which he believed challenged not only his own well-being but also that of other teachers. And so, after exhausting all possible remedies within his organization, he decided that whistle blowing was the only answer.

Tom's experience certainly does not support any argument that loyalty to an employer or a work organization is unimportant. On the contrary, loyalty is one of the highest virtues that a working Christian can cultivate. For without loyalty there can be no trust relationship between employer and employee, no true human involvement or potential for love.

But this incident does illustrate that on certain unusual occasions a Christian may find that some job problems come into such violent conflict with his own moral principles that he must take drastic action to correct the situation. Some Christians might disagree with Tom. They might choose simply to complain to the principal and, when that failed, resign with no further action. But Christians may also be called to assume a prophetic role. We may have to take a personal risk, which could endanger family finances or professional reputation, by speaking out against practices that we know are dangerous or wrong. For after all, the highest trust or loyalty that we owe is to God, who gives us access to a moral truth which demands our ultimate allegiance.

8
Don't Forget to Forgive

BOSS   "Gee, I'm really sorry I bawled you out yesterday. I was in a bad mood and didn't stop to think before I yelled."
EMPLOYEE   "That's okay, Mr. Jones."
BOSS   "Well, I just hope you can forgive me after all that profanity I used. There was no excuse for that, and I'll try not to let it happen again."
EMPLOYEE   "There's no problem, Mr. Jones. I just appreciate your concern."

Can you imagine such a conversation in any modern business office? Forgiveness, an uncomfortable virtue even among family and friends, blooms like a flower in a cold closet at work. Job success and achievement are commonly associated with a will to power, an ability to lead and control others. A forgiving act implies just the opposite because the person who forgives must give up a position of moral superiority over the one who has committed the wrong. In pardoning another, we say, "Your action is forgotten. We're on equal ethical terms again. I'm no longer the person who was wronged, nor are you guilty in my eyes of committing a wrong."

It's even harder for a workingman to confess his own wrongful act to a colleague. The person who *asks* forgiveness has to admit he was at fault and thus opens himself up to rejection or possible ridicule. He places himself at the mercy of a co-worker by saying, "Look, I know I treated you badly, but I want to apologize. Will you forgive me and let me know if there's anything I can do to set things straight?"

This vulnerability, or loss of power, makes forgiveness embarrassing and unpopular because we like to maintain protective shields around us. We want to fend off the efforts of other human beings to get too close to us, for they may expose our weaknesses and perhaps threaten our success potential.

But for Christians who regard personal relationships as the key to a rewarding, satisfying life, forgiveness is often an essential first step in repairing emotional injury and restoring friendship. The New Testament is laced with exhortations to forgive and seek forgiveness. Paul, in Ephesians 4:32, said, ". . . be kind to one another, tenderhearted, forgiving one another, as God in Christ forgave you." Jesus, in the Sermon on the Mount, taught that ". . . if you are offering your gift at the altar, and there remember that your brother has something against you, leave your gift . . . and go; first be reconciled to your brother, and then come and offer your gift" (Matthew 5:23,24). Jesus also illustrated the importance of seeking forgiveness in his parables. In the story of the prodigal son, for example, a young man took his inheritance and squandered it on immoral living. But realizing later that he was wrong, he returned contritely to his father and admitted, "Father, I have sinned against heaven and before you; I am no longer worthy to be called your son" (Luke 15:21). His father then forgave him and reinstated him to his former status.

But perhaps the most striking biblical example of a person

seeking to right his wrongs is that of Zacchaeus, the chief tax collector of Jericho. When Jesus stayed one day at Zacchaeus's home, the little tax collector repented of his unethical business practices: " 'Behold, Lord, the half of my goods I give to the poor,' " he exclaimed. " 'And if I have defrauded any one of anything, I restore it fourfold' " (Luke 19:8).

"Today salvation has come to this house," Jesus replied (Luke 19:9).

But the practice of seeking forgiveness for misdeeds at work is not limited to New Testament times. Ralph, a junior-high-school teacher whose students are mostly children of lower-income, poorly educated parents, has incorporated the uncomfortable virtue of forgiveness as a regular part of his teaching techniques. One day, a note was sent from the principal's office to ask a girl who was hard of hearing to leave the class temporarily for some reason. "She sat in the front row in this class and had to turn her head sideways so she could hear what was being said," Ralph explained. "But she definitely wasn't an abnormal personality or a freak."

"Here's a pass to the office, Jenny," Ralph called out. "Please come up and get it."

But she failed to hear him at first, and a student named John who sat next to her said loudly, "Yeah, weirdo."

Ralph immediately lost his temper. "Comments like that are despicable!" he shouted. "John, you must have been raised as a savage. You students are inhuman. Apparently you haven't learned the first thing about manners and how to treat other people. Don't your parents teach you anything about common decency? I warn you, another remark like that and I'll throw you bodily out of this class!"

The class fell completely silent, and many of the students

were apparently mystified at the outburst because they had not even heard the "weirdo" remark. The offending student, John, was almost in tears by the time the teacher had finished his tirade. A few minutes later, after he had simmered down, Ralph realized that he had overreacted and had so frightened his students that he had failed to get his main point across: That it is cruel and unfeeling for one student to ridicule the physical deficiencies of another.

"All right, I'm sorry I spoke angrily like that to the entire class," Ralph finally announced. "Most of you are basically kind and would never consider ridiculing another student. But remarks like the one John made—and I won't repeat it, we'll just forget it now—make me angry very easily. It's callous and cruel to poke fun at someone who's not as fortunate as you are. If another person has a physical disability, or has less money, or is not as athletic or as good a student as you are, you should help, not ridicule him.

"I should have taken this matter up with the offending student and not with the whole class, and I want to apologize for saying that you are not well brought up and that you don't care about other people. But let me remind you, John, and those of you who heard his remark, that even though I'm not shouting and raving now, I am very displeased. I won't tolerate that kind of abuse, and if it happens again, whoever is responsible will be punished."

Ralph then dropped the subject and returned to his lesson.

"I'm still sorry I blew my top, and I suppose making those remarks about their bad upbringing may have turned some of the students against me permanently," he said several weeks later. "Many of them came from bad family backgrounds, and it was unfair, even cruel of me to remind them of that, especially when most of them had done nothing wrong. But I think I repaired most of the damage by apologizing to them. If I hadn't felt free to say, 'I'm sorry,' I suspect my dealings with them during the rest of that semester would have been much more difficult.

"As a general rule, I think all workers, teachers included, should be able to be human and say, 'I've made a mistake.' An ability to ask forgiveness can definitely create a better rapport with a student. If I've been abusive or unfair to them, I say I'm sorry. I think that's basic to the Christian ethic. It's a model for confession, to be able to say in effect, 'I'm a sinner, please forgive me.' And by admitting that I'm wrong, I'm better able to turn a bad, bitter situation into a moral lesson, a constructive experience."

A Philadelphia insurance salesman named Jack related a similar experience to me. He said that a friend, Herb, had been wondering whether to incorporate his carpeting business and wanted to get some information on the insurance implications of setting up pension plans and other fringe-benefit programs.

"Herb was a heavy drinker and had a lot of family problems at the time," Jack explained. "His wife was on the verge of leaving him and his son was involved with drugs. Herb was basically a very unhappy guy, but a guy that I happened to like a lot. I've known him since we were kids together in high school, and I'd say we were very close friends."

Jack spent a considerable amount of his free time investigating Herb's business situation and finally advised him that it would not be profitable to buy any insurance until he actually took the steps to incorporate. Jack also recommended a good corporation attorney in case Herb finally decided to set up a corporation. Six months later, Jack learned inadvertently that his friend had incorporated his business, had used the suggested attorney, but had purchased his insurance from another agent.

"I was very, very upset, and my initial reaction was quite strong," Jack told me. "I was really hurt, and it was not because of the money I had lost either. I could have earned several thousand dollars in commissions, and that was a lot of money, but the important thing was that I had felt close to Herb. It was damaging to me personally."

In a fit of anger, Jack picked up the phone and bawled Herb out for taking advantage of their friendship.

"You made the initial contact with me, didn't you, Herb?" Jack said.

"Sure, Jack, but. . . ."

"I went over to see you on several occasions and counseled with you, and you followed some of that advice. Now, I would certainly think you have enough confidence in me to know that I could guide you in your insurance purchases as well as any other guy. You told me before any action was taken that you would notify me, but you didn't do that. You cut me out completely. Did you think I wouldn't find out? I don't understand you at all, Herb, not at all."

Herb, his voice quavering, was obviously distraught. "I'm sorry, Jack, I'm really sorry," he said.

With that, Jack hung up.

"But then I started to think about it," Jack said. "I worried about our conversation for most of that night. I felt much worse after that phone call—yes, I felt really horrible. And so I sat down the next day and wrote him a letter. I just told him that I had spoken in anger and haste and had been punished severely for it by remorse. I asked him for his forgiveness in the letter and said, 'I hope to see you again soon.' I don't know if our relationship will ever be the same, but I think that an apology was a necessary first step in trying to repair the damage that had been done."

Although a reprimand might have been appropriate for another person who had been so inconsiderate, Jack felt that, in Herb's case, "The scolding was totally unfair on my part. The incident was finished, and nothing positive could have been accomplished by venting my spleen like that. Besides, Herb is a very disturbed guy, with his drinking and personal problems. I should have been helping him, not putting him in that kind of box. Nothing was accomplished by making him feel horrible, and I definitely did make him feel like dirt. Sure, I had helped him on a professional basis, but I was mainly helping him as a friend. I shouldn't have expected anything in return under those circumstances. Otherwise, what are friends for? Why should I have damaged him just because I was hurt? It was against what Christ would want me to do, to maliciously hit a guy like that.

"But you know, it's great to be free enough to do what I finally did with Herb, to ask him to pardon my actions. Christ made me free enough to see that Herb was the same guy he was before he hurt me and to see that he needed my help. If my ego has been hurt and I have to retaliate, then I'm a captive, a prisoner to my own emotions of revenge. And I'm dependent on the acts of others, too, if I feel compelled to react in a certain way every time someone does something to me. But through Christ, I have the freedom not to be bound, not to lash out vindictively at another human being."

A vengeful, unforgiving attitude is a force to be reckoned with on the job, especially if the vindictive worker develops the reputation that he's "not a person you want to cross." But the experiences of Jack and Ralph show that, paradoxically, the vulnerability of forgiveness can also give an individual a certain power at work, a freedom to act outside the usual behavior patterns that create so many human problems.

Whether the forgiving or the unforgiving person is more likely to be a success in worldly terms is a matter for conjecture and is really irrelevant as far as the Christian is concerned. For the Christian lives with the assumption that the most important thing in life is the triangular love relationship between himself and other human beings and God. The power to forgive is an essential tool in overhauling and restoring human relationships when the destructive forces of self-interest, impulsiveness, and pride occasionally threaten to rip apart the often delicate harmonies achieved by love.

9
Witnessing at Work

"What do you think about this stock issue idea, John?"
"It's all right, Joe, but I think we should stick to the convertible preferred instead of the common."
"You may be right. By the way, do you know God loves you and wants to save you from sin?"

An exchange like this is the pet nightmare of many Christians who think that all explicit witnessing on the job must result in an abrupt, artless sales pitch. "There's a time and a place for everything," they argue. "You're not paid to preach in the office. It's just not appropriate."

Even those who acknowledge that witnessing is sometimes appropriate at work will often refrain from participating themselves for one of two reasons: Either they're afraid to put their faith on the line because of the possibility that a colleague may ridicule them or respond with some unanswerable question—or they're just plain lazy.

But Jesus refused to condone these passive attitudes and commanded us to witness actively to our non-Christian acquaintances on at least two levels. In the first place, we must communicate explicitly, through words: ". . . every one who acknowledges me before men, I also will acknowledge before my Father who is in heaven," Jesus said, "but whoever denies me before men, I also will deny before my Father who is in heaven" (Matthew 10:32,33). And the Apostle Peter wrote, "Always be prepared to make a defense to any one who calls you to account for the hope that is in you, yet do it with gentleness and reverence" (1 Peter 3:15).

The other level of witnessing, which is more subtle but just as important, involves communicating the power of the Christian faith by leading a moral, Christian life. Jesus said, "Let your light so shine before men, that they may see your good works and give glory to your Father who is in heaven" (Matthew 5:16).

"One of the main problems in talking to other workers about your faith is that you have to work with them eight hours a day," a New York construction worker said. "In one firm I worked for, I tried to witness to the guys who worked close to me, but it was almost futile, really. Nobody would really reject what I was saying. But it was a case of them saying, 'Yeah, yeah, yeah.' In other words, they *yessed* me to death. It was a nice way of saying, 'Don't bother me, willya?' After getting this treatment just so many times, you don't harass a guy any longer. You get on their nerves if you push them too hard, and that makes it tough to work together day in and day out. Besides, when a guy says *yes* to you and agrees with everything you say, what do you do after that? Call him a liar?

"I've found that God shows me the people he wants me to talk to. I don't have to bug everybody about my faith. There was this one fellow who sometimes ate lunch with me. He liked to discuss stuff, you know, was open to any kind of debate. Talking to him wasn't hard, and he never *yessed* me to death. Besides, he was in some trouble at the time, had some personal problems with his wife. Well, I started describing all this stuff about Christianity that he never knew before. I always kept it personal, told him what Christ had meant to me in my own life. And as simply as I could, I related my own experiences to biblical authority: I said man is in a sinful state, separated from God. Christ lived, was crucified, and rose from the dead to provide man with a way to overcome that separation and get into harmony with God. All you have to do is accept the fact that Christ lives and make him the master of your life. Then you'll have a direction, an ultimate meaning in your life because the power of God will grow in you each day.

"But I didn't push it. I just laid it out for him and we discussed the whole thing in detail until he understood. I told him he should go to a church in his neighborhood, and I suggested one with a minister I thought would be helpful. He went the next Sunday, talked to the minister, and decided to become a Christian. It was all so natural. No hassle."

Pat Worden, a former Brookline, Massachusetts, teacher, also said that she preferred to communicate her faith through well-established personal relationships. "My attitude on the job was one of friendship evangelism. My fellow teachers knew me as a person who was a real human being. When I discussed the gospel, I didn't push it on anybody because that would have been unreal. After all, I was interacting daily with those people."

But when a Christian gets explicit about the gospel with a fellow worker, he may find his words being tossed back in his face as pure hypocrisy unless his daily actions have supported what he says he believes. It's at this point that the two kinds of witnessing reinforce each other and give meaning to the biblical warning that ". . . faith apart from works is dead" (James 2:26).

For example, Mr. Smith, a big churchgoer who ran a Chicago warehouse, had a habit of throwing Bible verses and moral accusations around in an effort to convert his employees. If an employee made a mistake, he would typically say, "Well, I'm afraid you're not ever going to get your life straightened out if you don't trust the Lord. You're going to have to put the Lord in your life or you'll continue to have trouble."

Unfortunately, Mr. Smith was given to fits of anger when a subordinate displeased him, and his method of discipline was to humiliate the offending employee in front of his co-workers. His concern for the personal welfare of his workers can be illustrated by this incident: One day a young warehouseman came in to talk to Mr. Smith about a crisis that had struck him at home.

"My wife just left me, Mr. Smith, and I don't know who to turn to," he said, the tears rolling down his cheeks. "We have two little kids at home and there's no one to take care of them. Both of my folks are dead, and hers don't care what happens."

"Uh huh, that's too bad," Smith replied.

"I mean, I know I shouldn't be bothering you with this, but I don't know anybody else I can go to."

"Uh huh. Say, by the way, let me take a look at that hair. You know there's a rule about length of hair around here. I'm afraid I'm going to have to suspend you until you get that hair cut."

"But Mr. Smith, I just got it cut."

"Yeah, but you haven't cut it to meet our regulations."

"But Mr. Smith, I can't afford to go out and spend another $2.50."

"Sorry. And don't come back here until it's cut," Smith said and turned away from the boy without further reference to the personal problem that had started their conversation.

The next day, the young man, with his hair practically shorn, stamped into Smith's office. "Mr. Smith, I just have one thing to say to you," he declared. "Don't you ever, ever mention the word *Christianity* to me again!"

A Christian woman who worked for Smith as a secretary said that she thought her main purpose in the office was to be a counterexample to Smith so that the non-Christian workers would realize that not all believers acted as he did. "I've seen evidence that my life has had a chain effect, down to the lowest worker," she said. "One man went to church a few weeks ago just because of a casual remark I made to him. I met him on the street outside my church and said, 'Drop in to see us some time.' The next time I saw him he said, 'Hey, I did go to your church, you know.'

"I try to relate to people at work on a one-to-one basis through friendship. It's such a contrast with the way that Mr. Smith treats them, that I think some of them are beginning to think Christianity isn't so bad after all. One girl at work was having a lot of problems as it turned out because she'd gotten involved with a married man. She wanted to get out of that mess but didn't know how to handle the situation. I guess she figured that because I was older, I might know more about what to do. She sort of identified with me as an older sister. Well, we went out to dinner several evenings and she came to a few of my church activities. She was trying to make a break with this married guy, and I was the first one who had been concerned enough to encourage her. We're still seeing each other as friends, but I'm not pushing her. I try to tread lightly because she's not ready to commit her life. Somehow I have to get it across to her that being a Christian doesn't mean that you have to rule out having a good time.

"And I've done a lot of indirect witnessing that I think a Christian should do on the job. I've visited people in the hospital, been to two or three funerals. The people at work know I care for them and they have a pretty good idea about what I believe. Even though it can be sheer misery working for Mr. Smith, I think that God has intended for me to be here, if for no other reason than to demonstrate that not all Christians behave like our boss."

A similar approach was employed by a controller for a chain of grocery stores who told me about a series of discussions he had with one of his secretaries. "I noticed that she had problems getting along with some other people in the office," he explained. "I called her in and asked what the trouble was, if there was anything she'd like to discuss with me. She immediately told me about some family troubles she was having, and we hashed them out together.

"I took time on a couple of occasions to talk to her, and I think she felt comfortable because I try to get work out of my employees by encouraging them to come to see me if they have problems. I like to establish a personal relationship with each person under me, and it makes all the difference in the world when you try to communicate with them.

Our office staff is rather small, and I suppose it might be harder in a larger office.

"I know there are times when an employee takes advantage of me because I show an interest, but I think most of them trust and respect me. And the disadvantages are far outweighed by the advantages of being able to help people who need advice or guidance."

This controller said the secretary mentioned religion before he even thought of bringing the subject up. "She asked me about my faith, and it was natural for me to explain about Christ and what he's done for me. I finally told her that one way to take care of most of her problems, to get rid of the anxieties she was experiencing, was to turn her problems over to the Lord. She eventually became a Christian, and I think her commitment was genuine. She got along with the other employees much better and finally stopped consulting with me about her family situation, which she told me had improved."

Any boss who tries to witness to his subordinates will face a ticklish situation because of the natural tendency of some workers to use an employer's compassion for their own insincere purposes. But if the employee inquires about Christianity, isn't the supervisor in most instances bound to respond? Otherwise, he may be ignoring a genuine cry for spiritual help, a cry which may come only once or may be heard by no Christian other than himself.

A basic principle in witnessing for both employers and employees is illustrated in the experience of a Miami primary-school teacher: "The most fruitful way of witnessing to a person is to relate Christ's message to the individual's deepest need or interest," she said. "For example, one

teacher I worked with was agnostic, but she was interested
in all sorts of religions—Zen Buddhism, Christianity, you
name it. She was drawn to the intellectual side of Christianity, and I was able to spell out the gospel clearly for her in
the context of discussions about comparative religions.

"On another occasion, a good friend of mine, also a
teacher, had an operation for cancer, and I spent a lot of
time with her while she was recuperating. She wasn't as
interested in philosophizing as she was in wrestling with real
gut issues, matters of life and death. I spent a lot of time with
her after school, just keeping her company, and I tried to be
completely honest with her. I let her know about the frustrations I felt at school, and we shared mutual feelings about
work and life in general. She knew about my Christian commitment, of course: I was quite clear in explaining it to her
over the years. But I could never have pressured her to
commit herself because she was obviously not receptive to
that kind of approach."

This Christian woman concluded, "With some people
you can be straightforward: they want to know, and you can
lay the way to salvation out for them without hesitation. But
with most people, you have to decide you're going to establish a long-term relationship. Christ will give you a genuine
concern for their needs as human beings, and then as your
relationship develops over several weeks or months, Christ
reveals himself and his claims through you. Some people are
interested in knowing more about your faith. Others, though
they remain your good friends, are not. It's all quite natural."

There are thus a variety of ways to approach non-Christians with the message of the gospel, and no one way can

possibly be appropriate to every person and situation. The only constant factor in witnessing is that we have been commanded by Christ to do it in some fashion. The two ways of witnessing, by works and by words, will become natural and easy as we commit our way to the Lord and allow him to act through us.

10
Beating Boredom

Every generation of workingmen seems to encounter at least one crucial roadblock in the quest for job satisfaction. For many nineteenth-century factory workers, the main obstacles were long hours and inhuman working conditions. For the Great Depression generation of the 1930s, employment was either highly unstable or nonexistent.

But today a new threat to occupational happiness is competing for first place as the worker's most dreaded enemy. That's the challenge of boredom. Most of us spend the majority of our waking hours laboring at some occupation, and if those hours are unbearably dull, our entire outlook on life, including our inner sense of meaning, must suffer.

Countless words have been written about boredom on the job, but the solutions offered are never entirely satisfactory. *The New York Times* on February 5, 1973, carried an article on an experimental project to combat boredom by rotating job assignments at the General Foods pet food plant in Topeka, Kansas. Some of the workers found that the rotation technique broke the dull routine and made the job more interesting. But there were objections that these reforms are based on faulty, overly optimistic assumptions about human nature: Many of the new antiboredom programs stem from the idea that the average worker is not

primarily interested in higher pay, fringe benefits, and working conditions. Instead, according to these assumptions,
what the worker wants most out of a job is to be challenged,
to develop his innate human talents.

In the absence of a definitive solution that can solve the
problem for everyone, most of us are still left to combat
boredom in our own personal ways. And for the Christian
this usually means discovering some unique individual combination of practical expedients and Christian principles.

Sometimes, it may seem that the best solution to a boring
job is to quit, and Michael, an accountant from Michigan,
found that his Christian commitment was a decisive factor
in determining the way that he resigned. Michael had been
interested in a political job in Washington just before he
graduated from college, but he finally decided to join a
corporation in Detroit.

"I soon found that my accounting job, which mainly
involved keeping one portion of the books for the company's oil interests, was deadly," he said. "It was boring,
routine work, and it was also rather frustrating. The accountant before me had done a lousy job, and I had to correct
all his mistakes before I could properly evaluate the de-
preciation figures and other entries. Even when most of the
errors had been eliminated, I still felt that I was swamped
by meaningless figures. I never worked with a broad enough
section of the company's operations to see the big picture,
to see the forest instead of the trees. I was bored with the
job for about a year before I finally quit."

Michael explained that he had not been sure that he
wanted to work in a corporation in the first place, but he had
felt that he owed it to himself to give it a try since he had

spent four years as an accounting major in college.

"I would have left long before I did, but I had promised my boss that I would stay at least a year, and he was counting on my services for at least that long," he said. "In my opinion, a Christian has to honor commitments like that. It's a matter of being aboveboard and faithful in dealing with others. In this case, I tried to put the well-being of my boss above my own impatience to get out fast. But without the promise I had made, I would probably have left after about three months. I don't think you can tell about a job in the first day, or the first week, or even the first month. But I believe that if you still hate the job after three months and after prayer you don't see that any change is going to occur, then you should leave. Your boredom is a good indication from God that you should move on."

I can sympathize with Michael's attitudes toward boredom on the job because I faced just such a situation when I was at one West Coast duty station as a Marine Corps lawyer. My responsibilities included some interesting trial work, but there was also a great deal of routine, such as trying scores of guilty pleas and evaluating dull administrative discharges and investigations.

In an effort to escape this humdrum existence, I toyed with an idea that was regarded as anathema, even insane, for married reserve officers: I began to consider volunteering for duty in Vietnam. My wife Pam and I had many serious discussions about the issue, and I prayed frequently to ask God to give me guidance. There were many problems with serving in Vietnam. In the first place, an assignment in a combat zone, no matter how soft, would be more dangerous than weekends on the California beaches. Also, Pam and I would have to be separated from each other for the greater part of a year. But on the positive side, Pam, who had an interest in Japan, would get a chance—perhaps the only such opportunity she would ever have—to spend the year with friends in Tokyo.

Realizing that a risk was involved—that I might get an assignment I would dislike far more than my California position—I nevertheless decided to volunteer and was sent to the First Marine Aircraft Wing in Da Nang. Looking back on the experience, I'm convinced that God wanted me to do exactly what I did. On a strictly secular level, there was a greater variety of interesting cases in Vietnam and opportunities for travel in the Far East. But beyond these considerations, there were also many possibilities for spiritual growth. A couple of close calls in rocket attacks, for example, confronted me for the first time in immediate, personal terms with the meaning of death.

The Vietnam experience also unexpectedly enriched our marriage relationship. Being separated, which resulted in the breakup of many marriages, was a strain at first for us, as it is for many management consultants, salesmen, and other workers who are constantly away from home. But after a couple of misunderstandings, we learned a deeper meaning of trust and loyalty in marriage than I think would have been possible if I had failed to switch duty stations.

But changing jobs or duty stations is not always a feasible solution to the problem of boredom. An employee may face the loss of pension credits or other benefits which may be essential to his future or that of his family. Or the only alternative to a dull job may be another, equally dull job. When the choices of the Christian worker are limited like this, the best solution seems to be stressing personal relationships on the job and relying on game playing of some kind to break the monotony.

One assembly-line worker in a machine factory described his work as "pretty much the same thing every day, with only a few small variations. The only thing that makes it pleasant is if you're with a nice bunch of guys and you can kid and joke while you're working. You don't mind it so much as long as other people in the same position are nearby. But if you were working by yourself, you'd soon go out of your mind.

"My boss doesn't mind if we get up once every hour and take a smoke or something, to break the routine. We kid around, joke, talk about yesterday's ball game. Sometimes we'll even play some kind of word game while we're working. No one minds so long as you finish your work. And they always know if you get behind. Machine parts are constantly being brought in to me so I can do some work on them, and I have to keep up with the production schedule.

"Frankly, I find the actual work boring. But the guys I work with are great, and that alleviates a lot of the boredom problems. And our on-the-job relationships act as a starting point for getting together after work in situations where you can build closer friendships; knock around some ideas and beliefs that really matter. I never really dread going to work because I know I'll enjoy the company of these fellows. There's never silence, always a continuous discussion going on, even though our heads are down looking at what we're working on. This sort of friendly interaction and fooling around is absolutely necessary on my kind of job, and the boss knows it. If we sat there without talking for eight straight hours, we'd go nuts."

The experience of this Christian laborer suggests a basic truth about all kinds of job dissatisfaction: No matter how inherently interesting our work may be, if our lives focus exclusively on daily tasks, we are quite likely to become victims of boredom, frustration, or meaninglessness. But if the primary focus of a person's life is on Jesus, on how God can provide the power to build deep, loving relationships with other people, then boredom and other such complaints will assume less importance. Nearly every job—whether in the office or at home, as the next chapter will show—is boring to some extent. But God can provide the Christian with a new perspective so that the office or factory will be dominated by human beings who can enrich life rather than by impersonal machinery, deadening paper work, or monotonous assembly lines.

11
Christianity and the Working Woman
At Home

"Just a housewife"—these derogatory words have been used too often in recent years to describe one of the most important of occupations. This job, which I call *homemaker* because *housewife* fails to convey the significance of the motherhood role, has lost stature for several reasons, not the least of which is the barrage of criticism from Women's Liberation advocates.

I, for one, believe that the Women's Lib emphasis on women's rights, such as equal employment opportunities, is a good thing. But it's unjust to make the homemaker the fall gal, or the symbol of all that is wrong with the woman's status in our society. In short, I think it's time we restored the homemaker to the honored career status she deserves.

The specialized job of the homemaker is an ancient profession. In Proverbs 31, for example, the "good wife" is praised for her loyalty to her husband, her household management ability, her skill as a seamstress, her ability to market homemade products, her charitable interests, and her devotion as a mother. And I'm convinced that a woman who is a homemaker today is pursuing a career that is potentially every bit as valid as that of the lawyer, physician, secretary, or construction worker. I say *potentially* valid

because the unstructured hours associated with the job encourage some women to abuse their freedom, just as an
employee for some company may abuse a lenient company
policy. Some homemakers, in other words, become bums,
choosing to be lazy and unproductive rather than fulfilling
their potential in their chosen field.

What, exactly, are the homemaker's duties? According to
the women I spoke to, the central responsibility is motherhood. In fact, for most women, children are essential to
justify the very existence of the job. There are probably
exceptions to this rule, such as the politician's wife who
stays home to fulfill her duties as hostess if her husband is
committed to a considerable amount of entertaining. But
many women seem to agree that cleaning the house, shopping, and preparing the food are not sufficient reasons in
themselves for staying at home.

Some modern Christian wives tend to think in terms of a
career as a homemaker that spans a limited period of time.
One approach is to measure the mother's full-time responsibilities from the birth of the first child until the youngest
child reaches school age. Thus, a woman with two children
who were born two years apart would have a career commitment of eight years (six years for the first child to enter
first grade plus another two years for the second to reach
that level). When the kids are all in school, the mother often
feels more comfortable going to work part-time or full time
or getting involved in some other activity outside the home.

One strong argument for regarding the homemaker's role
as a full-fledged career is that the homemaker constantly
confronts problems that are similar to those faced by workers in any field. Perhaps the most serious difficulty for the

homemaker is the issue we discussed in the preceding chapter: how to handle boredom.

"The routine of housework can be very boring, especially when you have some basis of comparison with jobs outside the home," a Cleveland housewife named Ellen said. "If I didn't have my two children, I would definitely be working. I was a teacher before the kids were born. But I'm willing to put up with the boredom because I have the feeling that this is where God wants me at this particular time. This is what I think I should be doing.

"When I first quit teaching, there was no problem because everything was new: It was a complete change from what I'd been doing in the classroom. I got involved in stimulating neighborhood Bible studies with some other women, and did a lot of counseling and tutoring with other women. These activities made my days pretty full. It's only in the last two or three years, since we've moved from the suburbs to the city, that I've felt bored. I think the pressure of Women's Lib has been responsible for some of my dissatisfaction. But it's also a matter of doing the same thing for so many years—it's been nearly ten years for me now. My little girl will be in the first grade next year, and I'm already sending applications around for teaching jobs.

"I still participate in a lot of outside activities, including a reading and discussion group. I keep up on current literature and get together regularly with other women who are quite literate and sometimes working professionals. There's a lot of diversion from the household routine, but now I've reached the stage where I want to do something that's more substantial, more demanding. I'm tired of being home all day long."

Ellen explained that the full impact of the monotony of her household chores hits her with the cleaning duties. "It's so routine. The first time you clean a room, it's a challenge and you do a thorough job and it looks great. But when the house gets grubby again two or three hours later, I get frustrated. A certain amount of resentment builds up against my kids and my husband and myself because we're all so sloppy. Yet I get a contrary feeling that says, 'Look, I don't want to be mean, I don't want to make home a place where I'm griping all the time.'

"Sometimes it just gets to me, and I don't do anything for a day or two that doesn't just have to be done. Other days, I get ambitious and work until 11 o'clock in the evening. One time last spring I got so fired up that I decided to get completely organized and write down everything I should do in order to become the perfect housewife. I set up a chart of chores and worked very hard to complete them each day. I found it was possible to do everything I thought should be done, but I finally decided it wasn't worth the effort. I don't think anybody but me really cared whether my refrigerator was spotless or whether I had dusted under the beds each day."

Admitting that she doesn't "always combat boredom awfully well," Ellen has decided that "it's an unavoidable result of my decision to stay home at this stage with the kids. I do pray about my frustrations because they affect my relations with the other members of the family. I often will pray, 'Dear God, I'm really fouling this up, I'm acting improperly. Help me to act differently.' And God does help, prayer does make a difference.

"My Christian faith makes my feelings and emotions and

my analysis of household frustrations more complicated. If I were not a Christian, I might be tempted to say, 'Who cares about everybody else! I'm going to do what I want to do, and I don't care how the chips fall.' But because I am a Christian, I do care how the chips fall. I care about how my feelings affect other people, and I know if I'm frustrated and bored it's going to show, it's going to be communicated to my kids and my husband.''

Besides her discussions with other women, Ellen relies in part on other little diversions to take her mind off the monotony. "For example, if I have to iron, I'll try to do it while I'm watching a television talk show. And I'll break up my day by doing a certain amount of housework and then sitting down to read for a while."

But Ellen's best antidote to the monotony of household chores is her relationship with her children. "Cynthia, my youngest, comes home from nursery school at about 11:30 in the morning, and I feel a responsibility to know where she is and be available to her. I don't think hired help could do as good a job as I'm doing. The attitudes you convey and the way you act when a child is just learning to talk or when he's very young and has to be disciplined a great deal, are very important. I'd have great reservations about how well an outsider could guide the development of my child. In other words, a housekeeper might tell them that certain things are naughty, and I might not think they were naughty at all.

"Jonathan, my oldest, parrots back my values now, and if I weren't here he'd be doing that with the babysitter. I make a definite assumption that people matter. That goes back to my Christian orientation. I think it's important to give the kids some training in the insights I've learned into personal interactions. I'm influencing them with a certain set of values that I think are valid. If you want to exercise this kind of influence, you have to do it while they're young. And so I've decided I have to be with them at those early stages in their development for a significant part of each day."

But Ellen concedes that she does have certain "ambivalent feelings" about how much a parent should hover over her small children. She thinks that giving a child her undivided attention can be "both good and bad. If you jump every time they want something, you're going to produce kids who are very demanding of adults. These children really don't know how to entertain themselves or share adult attention. In short, they become spoiled. I try to make myself available to my kids, but at the same time I try not to overdo it and encroach on their independent development."

Kathleen Miller, a Dallas homemaker, feels very strongly that she was called by God at this stage in her life to work at home with her children. "I hear so many women complain that it's an empty life, that by raising children they aren't contributing anything to the world. They think they're wasting their time, and maybe, with that attitude, they are. Some people who are working as housewives definitely ought to be doing something else. But I think that being a homemaker is one of the most important jobs around in many ways. Look at the significant work that's involved: building a child's character, teaching him Christianity, encouraging him to have respect and love for others."

Before we leave our examination of the Christian

homemaker's role, a word of warning is in order: Nothing in this discussion should be taken to imply that husbands should avoid participating in household affairs. Most American families have not quite reached the "househusband" stage, where the man stays at home and the woman pursues a business career. But more husbands seem to be willing to help with the household chores even when the wife stays home all day to care for the kids. A few fathers are even taking paternity leaves from their jobs to stay at home for a while just after a child is born. And for the Christian father, some significant involvement with the kids is a necessity, as the Apostle Paul pointed out in Ephesians 6:4: "Fathers, do not provoke your children to anger, but bring them up in the discipline and instruction of the Lord." The impact of this increasing participation of men in household duties is especially significant in homes where both the husband and wife have outside jobs.

12
Christianity and the Working Woman in the Office

More and more women are deciding that they don't want to spend their entire adult lives in the home, and the result has been a surging increase of females in the job market. The 1970 national census revealed that two-thirds of the nearly twelve million new jobs that arose in the 1960s were filled by women. And the women's share of the total jobs in this country climbed from 32.7 percent in 1960 to 37.8 percent in 1970.

As women move into the working world outside the home, conflicts and changes have become inevitable both in the traditional husband-wife roles and in the way men and women relate to each other on the job. But the changes are sometimes slow to come, for many men resist recognizing the new status of their female co-workers and many women are hesitant to fight for equality on the job and at home.

Christian women are often the least aggressive in demanding their rights from their husbands and their male co-workers. They have consciously or unconsciously become wedded to the cultural context of the first century A.D., which is reflected throughout the New Testament. None of us would argue that because Jesus and the other early Christians are described as wearing sandals and robes that we must do likewise. Yet we are often much less certain when it comes to prohibitions against women speaking in church, or worshiping bareheaded, or being able to "have authority over men," a practice which the Apostle Paul discouraged in 1 Timothy 2:12.

Most of the Christian resistance to giving women more responsibility can be traced to Paul's teachings in his Epistles. Paul's attitudes sprang from a cultural context in which women were made subservient to men by law, and he even acknowledges this legal foundation in Romans 7:2: ". . . a married woman is bound by law to her husband as long as he lives; but if her husband dies she is discharged from the law concerning the husband." His teachings about the woman's role in the family, such as, "Wives, be subject to your husbands, as to the Lord" (Ephesians 5:22), must be considered in light of this legal and cultural context. If Paul had lived under another set of laws and customs, such as those in our society, would he have expressed his teachings about women in the same way? I think probably not.

In some letters to the churches, Paul was careful to use the first person pronoun in describing the role of women in the church: "*I desire* then that in every place the men should pray . . . also that women should adorn themselves modestly . . . by good deeds, as befits women who profess religion . . . *I permit* no woman to teach or to have authority over men; she is to keep silent" (1 Timothy 2:8-10, 12, emphasis supplied). Paul's choice of the first person suggests to me that he was expressing his own personal opinion about what was valid and appropriate for that historical period.

But whether this interpretation is correct or not, the apostle was clearly referring in those passages to the role of women in the Christian community, not to their roles in the working world. The question of the woman's proper role in the business community never arose because the concept of the career woman was apparently not an important social issue for Paul. In the Old Testament, on the other hand, the judge Deborah is a solid precedent for a woman to control an entire nation by transmitting the word of God and ordering troops into battle (*see* Judges 4).

As far as the status of modern women is concerned, the contemporary working world would seem closer to Deborah's time than to Paul's. For today there is an increasing tendency for women to seek work outside the home, and this tendency has affected the expectations and sensitivities of Christian women as well as non-Christians.

"For people of my generation, the rules have been changed in the middle of the game," declared Connie, a forty-year-old homemaker who is preparing to reenter the job market now that her children are in school. "When I was in college, the ideal was to get married. The Mrs. degree was as important as the B.A. It was a joke, but there was a lot of truth to it. It was always a big deal when somebody got engaged. I worked as a social worker before the kids came and I enjoyed it, but my own job aspirations had to remain compatible with my husband's. Besides, I didn't regard the work as something I was going to be doing permanently. My thinking was quite common for the 1950s. I regarded my husband's occupational position as all-important, and so I continued to work while he finished his graduate-school education.

"I wasn't unhappy playing by those old rules. I didn't feel

like I was being had, and I don't feel now that I've been had. The expectations were that you would center your life around your husband and your family. But now, all of a sudden, by both society's new rules and even by my husband's new attitudes, I should be doing more than just raising kids. I should have a life of my own outside the home, a career of my own. I need some specific training I don't have now, and so I'm planning on going back to school eventually. The new rules are that you have a life of your own and you become an independent person in your own right. You don't get your gratification just because your husband does such and such. You get gratification because *you* are doing such and such.

"At this stage, my husband and I are certainly not co-equals in career terms, but I think we could be. In retrospect, I wish a career had been more important to me when we first got married because I'm behind now and I have to do some catching up. As a practical matter, we'd starve if my husband quit work now and we had to rely on what I could make in the job market."

Connie noted that the scriptural references to women make her attitudes about her proper role in life "more complex and ambivalent. As a Christian, I want to do what honors God, and I believe that there is a validity to scriptural principles. I really haven't resolved these issues, and I suppose I'll be thinking and praying more about them as I prepare to go back to work. Covering your head and not speaking in church seem to me to be cultural things, not eternally valid principles. But just how far a woman can become like a man in the job world is something I haven't answered adequately for myself."

Despite the movement of women into the job market and

the growing concern with equal employment opportunities, female job hunters frequently encounter male job interviewers who are prejudiced against them because of their sex. "Most of the time we're interviewed for jobs by men," an unemployed female marketing specialist told me. "I think most men don't take you seriously. You know, their attitude is, 'Who are you, to ask to be something above a secretary?'"

As an example, she told how one personnel man evaluated her resume during an interview. Although there were references to a master's degree in economics and numerous jobs she had held as an administrator, he barely looked at those credentials before saying, "We don't have anything right now, unless you'd like to work on our telephone switchboard."

"How can I do that sort of job?" she asked. "Do you see 'switchboard operator' listed on my resume?"

"Well, no, but. . . ."

"But you thought I might be able to do that because I'm a woman? Would you have asked that question if I'd been a man?"

The interviewer, obviously flustered, shrugged, looked down at the resume, and was undoubtedly relieved when she walked out. Most Christians approach this discrimination problem like any other: First they keep constantly in touch with God through prayer. Then, when it seems appropriate, as it did to the woman in the above example, they act. They may confront the employer or prospective employer directly about his prejudice, or perhaps they will complain to the local human rights' office.

But when the Christian woman confronts her male supervisor with an injustice, she has to be careful that she plays by the male-established rules of the game. Otherwise, the effectiveness of her position may be weakened. Tears, for example, are generally regarded as the characteristic response of most women to a frustrating, difficult situation. But if the sobs come at the wrong moment, they can destroy the woman worker's leverage in a confrontation with her boss.

One public-school teacher named Jean said that she ran into this problem with her principal as a result of an edict he handed down on lunchroom practices. The principal, Mr. Hale, who was unpopular among the teachers and had developed a reputation in some quarters as being somewhat neurotic and incompetent, circulated a memo saying that the teachers could no longer eat with each other in the school cafeteria. Instead, they would be required to eat with the students, one teacher at each student table. He explained that there had been complaints about the way the children were behaving and that the teachers would thus have to exercise more discipline over them.

The state legislature had passed a law saying that teachers should be given an hour lunch break and that school aides should be hired to fill in the gap, but the legislators added a qualification that this provision was to be enforced only at local option. Despite the fact that her locality had not exercised this option, Jean felt that the very act of passing the law reflected a public concern that teachers should be given a break during the day. She also believed that, apart from the law, Mr. Hale's ruling was unjust. After several other teachers urged her to speak to the principal for them, she prepared her arguments on the issue and made an appointment with Mr. Hale.

Upon entering his office, Jean immediately got to the

point: "I hate to take your time, Mr. Hale, but there's a serious problem that's bothering many of the teachers and I want to call your attention to it."

"What's that?" he asked.

"Your rule that we have to eat with the students. Now, the general feeling is that this is unfair. In the first place, we do get worn out dealing with the students all day long in classes. Just for the sake of our morale and psychological well-being, I think it's important for us to have some time to ourselves in the middle of the day. You know, so we can unwind and relax and get ready for the afternoon classes. But in the second place, you're aware there was a law on this very issue that was passed by the state legislature, and that to me indicates a more general public concern with the issue. Now. . . ."

Mr. Hale, who had been wearing a disconcerting grin during her entire presentation, cut her off with a broad shrug: "Well now, Jean, if you dislike children so much that you can't even eat lunch with them, I'm wondering whether you're in the right field?"

"Why, that's incredible . . . I . . ." she sputtered angrily and finally broke into tears. "You just don't understand the teachers at all. You couldn't, issuing an order like that. I don't think you care one bit how we feel!"

"Why, I don't have a malevolent bone in my body for anyone, Jean."

"Well, I do!" she retorted.

After a few more words, most of which came from Mr. Hale in an effort to calm her down, Jean stamped out of the office. Thoroughly disheartened, she pondered her performance at home that evening and tried to evaluate where she had gone wrong.

"I felt so threatened and nervous before I went in to see him that I was incapable of seeing the game he was playing with me," she explained later. "He always tried to change the subject and put you on the defensive so that he wouldn't have to answer a valid complaint you might be making. I found out later that he wasn't all that courageous in confrontations with people, but I was too unsure of myself at that point to be able to understand him. I didn't have the personal maturity to know how to be more aggressive and cool headed in dealing with him. Instead, I got mad and ended up in tears."

This was a classic case, she admitted, of the dominant male overcoming the submissive female. And once the female had been defeated, the boss could become paternalistic with a statement like, "I don't have a malevolent bone in my body. . . ."

"As a Christian, I should have tried to understand him better, and I should have prayed more seriously before I went in to see him," she said. "As I recall, I prayed afterwards. And feeling badly about how I had handled the situation, I decided to write Mr. Hale a note. I apologized for having lost my temper, because I hate to lose control of myself in any personal relationship. I don't think God wants that. But I didn't take all the blame either. I told him in the note that I thought there was fault on both sides, and I quoted to him from a book on management practices. The selection in question stated that reasons should be given when changes are made and that the people affected should be notified and asked for their reactions. He had in effect broken every rule of proper administration, and I wanted to let him know in as nice a way as possible that I knew this. I gave him my reasons for being upset and explained that

I felt the situation could have been handled better by both of us. The note was both a justification of my position and also an apology for the way I had conducted myself.

"I disliked this man intensely and I had severe guilt feelings about my attitude. I knew it wasn't Christian, and I did pray for him and prayed for my relationship with him. Yet, although I don't think I ever completely mastered the relationship, I learned a lot from it. For one thing, I know now that a woman can't get mad and cry when she gets into a frustrating confrontation with a man because the result will rarely be to her advantage. My behavior certainly didn't help me."

As contemporary Christian women attempt to carve out meaningful positions for themselves in the job market, certain changes in the husband-wife relationship may also be necessary. For if the woman works the same hours outside the home as the man, there is a general feeling that she should be relieved of some of her household responsibilities. For some couples who have the financial means, hiring baby-sitters and housekeepers with the extra income provided by the wife may solve all these problems. But most people will find that they cannot afford to have everything done for them at home by a third party. And so the alternative is for the husband and wife to divide the chores and the care of the children between them.

An executive secretary who works for a West Coast company said she had worked for several years and at first had tried to do all the housework, shopping, and child care by herself. "I used to bottle things up, keep it all inside, never say a word about what I felt in these areas," she explained. "But I realized things were quite unfair, one-sided. Finally,

I decided that I had put up with enough and that the only way to have an understanding with my husband, John, about the problem was to bring it up. We had a couple of discussions and I tried to impress on him that I felt he should take on more of the domestic responsibilities. In effect, I told him, I had two full-time jobs. I do believe that the husband should be given respect and honor. But I also believe that marriage is a partnership, and John believes this way, too. I felt that I was being taken advantage of, that I wasn't really a full partner. There are many family matters on which his word should be taken as the final authority. But I also believe that we, as a Christian couple, are supposed to work together to achieve common goals, including the development of a good personal relationship and helping our sons to build solid Christian characters.

"And so we decided after our discussions that we'd split the chores around the house. We go to the grocery store about half or three-fourths of the time together. One time, while we were shopping, he told a clerk he had to go home and put one of the items in the freezer right away. The boy who was doing the packing said, 'You have to put the groceries away?' John said, 'No, I don't have to, but I do.' I think this was an eye-opener for this boy. He probably thought John was a henpecked husband."

In my own home we've adopted a similar arrangement because both my wife and I work. She cooks; I wash the dishes. I do the laundry and clean the bathroom; she vacuums and tidies up the rest of the apartment. I insist that she act as a domestic supervisor and assign the chores because I have a higher tolerance for household clutter than she does. If we had not agreed that she would be in charge of the cleanup detail with the authority to prod me into action, I would probably do nothing at all. She, on the other hand, would do much more than she does now and would undoubtedly become frustrated and overworked.

Each working couple has to settle on its own arrangement in this frontier region of marital relationships. There is no one correct answer, but whatever the final division of duties, there must be considerations of love and sacrifice on both sides. For even the Apostle Paul prefaces his ideas on the subjection of wives to their husbands with this command: "Be *subject to one another* out of reverence for Christ" (Ephesians 5:21, emphasis added). And he further admonishes the men, "Husbands, love your wives, as Christ loved the church and gave himself up for her . . ." (Ephesians 5:25). The marriage relationship, in other words, is a two-way street. The husband as well as the wife must labor and sacrifice if their love relationship is to grow and provide them both with a firm base to build productive Christian lives both at home and in the office.

13
For Professionals:
The Christian-Client Relationship

The professional man or woman occupies a position of exceptional personal power in our society. The independence, prestige, and high income potential of physicians, lawyers, and other such workers can enable them to achieve the wildest dreams of material success and sated self-interest.

But a professional occupation means something more than unqualified egomania for the Christian. The Christian professional, with his specialized education, often has opportunities to do good for his fellow man on a wider scale than the average company employee. This extra potential for good imposes additional responsibilities, including the need to be unusually self-disciplined and sensitive to the moral implications of daily tasks.

The need for inner discipline and ethical sensitivity is reflected in even the most mundane phases of the professional's work. For example, because there is often no one to oversee him, he may be tempted to cheat clients when he charges them for his services.

"I'm very conscientious about billing my clients," a clinical psychologist said. "If someone pays me for fifty minutes, I try to be sure that he gets his whole time from me. As a

Christian, I feel a strong responsibility for self-regulation. There's not an awful lot I can do to manage someone else's life, but there is a lot that I can do to manage my own. And by managing my life properly, I think I can have some effect on the ethical climate of society in general. A lot of people see the moral fiber of our country going downhill, and, thinking that nothing can be done to change things, they decide to cheat because other people do. But immorality can have a snowball effect, and I believe I have the power in my own little sphere to resist that tendency.

"When the wage-price freeze began in 1971, I could have raised my fees for the new patients who came to me after the freeze began. But I felt some responsibility for self-regulation. For me, that means taking the responsibility for your own behavior, taking into account the broader social impact of your individual actions. It's a matter of doing what you would want others to do. When I'm doing something lousy to somebody, I often ask myself whether I would want that done to me. Somehow, relating this back to the Golden Rule in the Sermon on the Mount (Matthew 7:12) sounds like a cliché. But that's really what it amounts to. It's a matter of considering what it would be like to be on the receiving end. If I keep a client waiting, I think myself what it might be like to be kept waiting. I believe other people's time is valuable, and so I try to keep strictly to a schedule. With some doctors, you might wait up to two or more hours in a waiting room, and I think that's wrong."

Some professionals, such as those who draw government salaries, may be tempted to compromise the quality of their services because their organization lacks supplies or adequate personnel. These professionals may complain once or twice to a boss, but then if their requested changes do not occur swiftly, they often just give up and accept mediocrity.

One physician who refused to make such a compromise was a Christian who worked in a federal clinic in an underprivileged neighborhood in Washington, D.C. "The administrators in charge of our program are incompetent," he said flatly. "Whoever is in charge of ordering medical supplies doesn't do it properly. They don't know how to stock materials, how to order them, how to anticipate shortages. And they overlook or forget many of our requests.

"For example, we need a drug to do skin tests for tuberculosis. The other doctors and I usually get together and estimate how many supplies we'll need for this test for a month in advance. Then we go to the administrators and say, 'Look, we anticipate we're going to see 150 patients this next month who will need skin tests. Order us 150 for that month.' But frequently we find out all of a sudden we're out of supplies. Some of my colleagues just shrug and don't give the tests, but I can't do that. I dig down into my own pocket and buy what I need. During the last month, I've spent sixty-five dollars of my own money for medical supplies. Without those materials, I couldn't have done an adequate job of caring for my patients.

"Many doctors have quit this job because of this problem, but I still think our relationships with the administrators, who are not physicians themselves, can be worked out. Besides, if I leave, what will happen to these needy patients? I may be financing the program out of my own pocket, and I certainly don't think that's right, but I plan to stick it out for a while to see if things can be changed for the better."

This doctor's sense of priorities is echoed in the experience of a lawyer, who subordinated his own interests to those of his fellow workers on a consumer-rights research project. "I've had several invitations to join law firms or other research projects at a higher salary," he said. "But I felt a sense of responsibility to the other people who are working on this project. I know that many other people wouldn't hesitate to leave this job for one that pays more, and it wouldn't necessarily be professionally reprehensible or unethical. But I operate under a different standard, a standard that has its roots in Christ's teachings about how we should treat one another. I try to see my life in relationship to that of other people. A Christian should have concern for others; become aware of their needs as well as his own. Sometimes, it's even a matter of making our own needs secondary, though I don't believe in always deferring to the wishes or needs of others in my career decisions. But I do try to remember at all times that my standard is Christ, who limited himself by choosing to be incarnated and then crucified. What greater self-limitation can there be than for God to become man?"

The special skills of the professional also provide him with powerful tools to help those who can't afford to help themselves. Just as the wealthy corporation executive may be able to contribute more money than any of his employees toward a good cause, so the professional may have the opportunity to donate his valuable services. This *pro bono publico* (for the public good) work is increasing among professionals, and some Christians are taking the lead in the movement.

"My Christian orientation to life has been very important in my decision to provide certain services for free," an experienced corporation attorney said. "For example, I set up a nonprofit foundation which has financed research into some areas of Christian history that had not been adequately studied. It took a lot of time and effort for me to do the legal work for the project, but I'm convinced it was worthwhile. We need this kind of research if our church is going to survive and flourish. And my time as an attorney is a much more valuable contribution than any money I might give.

"But when your time becomes very valuable, as it is for many professional people, then you have to start making value judgments. You can try and do everything that people ask you to do for them, but of course that's impossible. And so you find you have to be discriminating and seek guidance from God for your final decision."

This attorney said that determining what standards to use in setting priorities for *pro bono publico* work is "difficult because it's not only my time, it's also the time of younger lawyers who work under me." He explained that his policy is to allocate fees from his paying clients to young associates who are helping him with the charitable work. In that way, the young lawyers don't appear to be doing less work than their peers when earnings comparisons are made.

"These young guys are freeing me to do billed-out work at double the rate that they themselves would be able to charge," he said. "In this way, the firm doesn't lose my services for important paying clients who come to us with complex problems. My *pro bono* commitments often involve more routine legal research which is within the expertise of the less experienced lawyers."

This attorney also participates as a trustee for several

medical and educational centers, and he makes himself available when necessary to give legal advice to these institutions. "One wealthy real estate developer wanted to give us some land to expand our facilities for a children's hospital that I'm involved with," he said. "But we learned that the title to the land was not clear: Other people had claimed that they actually owned part of it as a result of some past land deal. I contributed a good deal of my own time and that of some of my interested young associate attorneys to straighten out the mess. We finally worked out an equitable settlement with the other claimants, but if we hadn't made the effort, the hospital might never have gotten the land. Or we might have acquired the property and then become embroiled in a lengthy, costly lawsuit.

"I feel very strongly about this particular hospital and the kind of work it's doing. Children don't ask to be born in the first place, and they certainly don't ask to have a crippling disease. The study of these diseases is very important, and some of the services offered by this hospital aren't available anywhere else."

This sense of concern both for individuals and for social betterment is, unfortunately, a characteristic of far too few professionals. In the past, many Americans were ready to believe that physicians, lawyers, and judges were worthy of respect and honor. But lately, we seem to be encountering an increasing number of lawyers who are convicted of bribery, judges who are lazy and incompetent, and doctors who defraud the public by cheating on Medicaid fees. The professional is in a position of power where he can do considerable evil or considerable good to his fellow man.

The imperative of the Christian faith requires that he take his potential for good seriously so that God's final evaluation of his work can echo Matthew 25:21: "Well done, good and faithful servant."

14
The Christian Man as a Union Man

Labor union leaders have acquired a bad name over the years in certain quarters. Ask a nonunion man what he thinks of the labor movement, and he may say something about the infiltration of organized crime, or mention the convictions against such stalwarts as former United Mine Workers' president William A. (Tony) Boyle and former Teamsters' boss James R. Hoffa. And the average consumer is becoming increasingly disenchanted because of charges that huge union wage settlements are forcing consumer prices up to unacceptable levels.

But despite these antiunion sentiments, the power wielded by labor leaders carries just as great a potential for good as the power of the professional person or the corporate executive. The Christian who is a member of a union and who feels he has a certain leadership potential must ask himself: Could I do a better job than the present union officers? If so, should I make a union office one of my goals on the job? One Christian who answered yes to both these questions was a fellow named Mack who worked in a northeastern printing plant. He decided that he should try to become a union officer when he noticed that the incumbents were not being forceful enough in trying to solve problems that many individual workers could not solve by themselves.

"Because I thought the officers in my union local weren't doing enough to help some of the workers, I often criticized the job they were doing," Mack said. "As a joke, sort of half-serious, a couple of guys asked me why didn't I run for vice-president. And so I took them up on it; I ran kind of as a lark. I put on a big razzle-dazzle campaign with posters and so forth, and my opponent started campaigning that way, too. Nobody had ever done that before, and we sort of woke up the whole plant. As it finally turned out, I beat the guy by four votes, and my first thought was, 'What do I do now?' "

Mack's first major encounter with union power politics involved a plant employees' contract that had expired and required renegotiation. He was chosen to be part of the negotiating team because he was known to be outspoken on job issues.

"I came to realize the whole thing was a big game," he said. "We came up with these fantastic demands in planning our negotiating strategy, but nobody expected us to achieve them: You know, double our old vacation time, 50 percent salary increase, and so on. Then, we went into the negotiating session and took seats around this big table and everyone knew it was all a big charade. We'd present our ridiculous demands and the company people knew ahead of time they were ridiculous, but they'd listen with these serious expressions on their faces.

"We had a union representative who was our spokes-man. Invariably this guy looked like a thug. He was a real Broderick Crawford type. We didn't have a lawyer, just this gangster who needed a shave and had egg stains on his shirt. When I met with this guy in the presence of the president and vice-president of the company, I almost wished I were on the other side."

Mack said that during his entire tenure as an officer, he had ambivalent feelings about the role of the union. He thought there was an evil aspect because "in a union you get what you can grab. The main purpose for some of the officers is to use the power of the organization selfishly to get as much power for themselves as they can.

"You could easily get your throat cut if you tried to bring up any Christian ideas or principles at a union meeting. For factory workers, the number one thing is 'I want to get all I can.' No matter how much you get, the feeling is always that the company can afford more, and so the moral thing to do is grab all that you can. Management, of course, will do the exact same thing. Then the two sides knock heads until they come up with something that both can live with. But the standard of righteousness for both sides is still how much you can get, no matter how you do it.

"I've seen the union representative lie through his teeth, falsify figures when he thought it would be to our advantage. Everybody on the negotiating team except me thought this was the right thing to do because we might get something from the company, which could afford it anyway. Of course the company negotiators would always catch the phony figures. It was all part of the charade.

"I guess you can't expect business institutions to operate on principles of personal Christian morality. Suppose I said at a union meeting, 'Look, fellows, you're not playing fair with these company guys. You said this, and now you're going to do that. You're lying to them, and that's not right.' The other members would say, 'You and your religion can

go and take a run. You're talking about my pocketbook.'
Money is of paramount importance to the worker. He
doesn't care about ethics or anything like that when it
comes to his wages. I was eventually voted out of office
because I objected to some of the more questionable union
practices and got the reputation of being a 'company
man.'"

These observations are reminiscent of the arguments of
Reinhold Niebuhr, in *Moral Man and Immoral Society,* that
two levels of morality exist in our society, one for the individual and another for the organization. The highest morality for the individual is based on love and unselfishness, but
selfishness is probably inevitable when men relate to each
other through groups. The natural selfishness of the special-
interest group can be countered and justice between groups
can be best achieved by applying the coercive power of an
opposing organization. But any attempt to impose individual
moral values on an organization is probably doomed to
failure. Thus, a selfish labor union, which wields the threat
of a strike, is the natural answer to the selfish company
tendency to force employees to work for low wages and
inadequate fringe benefits.

Despite the selfish orientation of unions, Mack believes
that "the fact that they exist is a good thing. I'm for a union,
put it that way, because it prevents a guy from getting
shafted at the company's whim. It protects the weak guys.
If a company consisted of committed Christians, I wouldn't
even suggest putting a union in there. But a worker is just
like a thing to a lot of company people, an inhuman object
to dispense with as they see fit. The guys in my company
have a merciless attitude toward the employees and their

problems. The union gives the workers a little more humanity. It enables us to be human beings. When you have a union, the company treats you a little more respectfully than if you didn't have one. In a union company, if someone has a grievance or a squawk, he gets treated courteously and his problem is looked into immediately. But without a union, the problem is ignored. I've worked in companies without a union, and I know. If you get shortchanged in your pay, they'll wait until you scream and then look at you as though they're doing you a big favor. But with a union, if I get shortchanged, I go to the foreman and he immediately gets on the phone and notifies the accounting office. He knows if he didn't, the shop steward would lodge a complaint."

Mack had several opportunities to use the power of his union position to force the company to give workers benefits that they might not have received otherwise. On one occasion, a young woman wanted her company medical insurance to pay certain expenses for her, but she was told by her boss that she had been absent from work for too many days during the quarter of the year in question to qualify for the benefits. Mack decided that this decision was unjust because the very reason the woman had missed the time at work was that she had been sick. And he learned that it would be the insurance company, not the employer, that would have to fork over the money.

Mack first went to the production manager who supervised the woman and argued, "For Pete's sake, the whole purpose of a medical program like this is to help people who are sick. How can you hold this woman's sickness against her in counting the days it takes to become eligible for benefits? If the company had to pay, I could see why you might oppose this. But it's an insurance issue. There's no reason for you not to try to help an employee in this case."

But the production manager, who had a reputation as the "number one evil guy in the company," denied the request by declaring flatly, "You got no case."

"You guys aren't even human," Mack retorted, and then he went to the office of the company vice-president, who eventually took him in to see the president.

"You know, you are all looking like bad guys, and it's all for nothing," Mack told the president. "Look, you have a chance to be a hero, and you're being a louse. This is insane. Remember LBJ said that if you can do something for someone and it doesn't cost you anything, do it, because you can always collect on it later. Now here you have a chance to be a hero, so do it. Why make yourself look like a bum when you don't gain anything by it? All you have to do is talk to the insurance company, and they'll pay. Otherwise, you gain the animosity of the people."

"Okay, but we'll have to make adjustments in the medical contract," the president replied.

"So make them," Mack said.

The president then called in the production manager, who had thrown a fit because Mack had gone over his head. "Look, they're making a big issue out of this, and it's not going to cost us anything," the president said. "Go along with them."

Mack said that his position in the union was strong enough that he was able to win this fight "almost single-handedly. I screamed and yelled and screamed and yelled and finally they made adjustments so that the girl got paid several hundred dollars. The company, as I had expected, didn't lose anything because they worked it out with the insurance people. They revised the rules after this so that the employee could benefit in the future if a similar situation arose.

"The company at the beginning had in effect said, 'We don't give a hoot about her,' and that bothered me. I learned it's not whether you're right or wrong as far as the company is concerned, but whether you yell enough. The company people finally get to the point where they listen to us because we always have the threat of calling in the union representative from the main union office. Then some thug would come up—you know, acting like Broderick Crawford. The company officers didn't want to have anything to do with this guy because he always caused headaches. They'd have to leave their comfortable offices and come down to listen to this baloney head for two hours. We always had the threat of calling in this guy, and I didn't hesitate to use it. I think one of the main things I contributed while I held union office was that I wasn't afraid to stand up to the executives and fight for an individual's rights."

The position of a union officer, then, is quite similar to that of a management supervisor, politician, or anyone else in a leadership role. Opportunities abound for abuse, for increasing one's own wealth and influence. But opportunities also abound for helping the weak and downtrodden, the ordinary workingmen who are still plugging away in their powerless jobs. Saul of Tarsus, a man of great leadership ability, was the spearhead of the attack by the Jewish religious community on the early Christians. But after his conversion on the road to Damascus, Saul, who afterwards went by his Roman name Paul, became the main advocate of the Christian faith and was instrumental in spreading the gospel throughout the Roman Empire. The Christian has a similar potential to do good on a broad scale through his labor organization if he seeks divine guidance and stays sensitive to the needs of fellow workers.

15
The Padded Expense Account:
A Study in the Art of Fair Stealing

Everybody is interested in earning more money because a higher salary makes it easier to pay the rent, put food on the table, and buy a few of the luxuries of life. But because employers have traditionally been reluctant to hand out raises, many workers are tempted to use unofficial channels to increase their earnings.

The ways in which employees try to augment their pay are ingenious and endless: They may use company stationery and stamps for private correspondence, or perhaps take an extra stapler home for their personal use. Some employees make unauthorized long-distance calls on company telephones. Others, despite larceny statutes, pad their expense accounts to get extra income.

A common argument is that it's all right to engage in such practices because "everyone does it." Noting that government authorities rarely enforce certain minor criminal laws relating to business, many employees claim that a custom of "fair stealing" has in effect replaced the laws.

The Christian approach to this fair stealing is not as simple and straightforward as might appear at first glance. We are told in the Ten Commandments that it's wrong to steal, and both Jesus and Paul affirmed this teaching in the New Testament. (*See* Matthew 19:18 and Romans 13:9.) Paul and Peter tell us to be subject to the "governing authorities" and to "every human institution" (Romans 13:1; 1 Peter 2:13). But does everyday business practice raise custom to the level of law, or to the same status as the "human institutions" that we are supposed to obey? More specifically, how far can the Christian legitimately go in increasing his income through these customary channels?

The answers to some of these questions may become clearer if we take a closer look at how individual Christians have handled the fair stealing problem. Perhaps the best case study involves one of the most common and lucrative forms of fair stealing—padding the company expense account.

Expense accounts are considered a part of the necessary operating expenses of any business. The company, in other words, provides funds to entertain prospective clients, to send employees on business trips, and to pay for cab rides from one business location to another. Reimbursements to the employees who entertain and travel qualify as tax deductible items for the employer under both federal and state laws. But this description only tells half the story. By tradition in many companies, another major function of the expense account is to provide opportunities for unofficial salary raises.

Basically speaking, there are two ways to steal fairly through an expense account. Under one method the employee must first ascertain the maximum expenses customarily associated with his job. He then spends the money allotted to him as lavishly as his company allows. But instead of trying to further the company's business interests, he indulges himself by taking unnecessary cab rides and buying lunches for friends. His expense reports reflect his actual expenditures, even though he benefits more than his employer.

The other stealing technique also requires the worker to determine the maximum expenses permitted for his job. But this worker falsifies his account by reporting the maximum allowable expenses while actually spending a smaller amount of money (e.g., he reports six dollars for a meal even though he actually spent only two dollars). The worker then pockets the difference in cash. Under the first fair stealing method, in other words, the employee gets the benefit immediately on the job, while under the second he enjoys himself later with his extra income.

Access to an expense account is usually associated with the higher echelons of management. And it is certainly true that corporation presidents and vice-presidents are more likely to have expense allowances of several hundred dollars a week than the average mail clerk or secretary. But lower-level workers, especially those who work as public relations representatives, salesmen, and purchasing agents, also often have expense accounts. And if it's the company custom to pad expenses, employees on every income level quickly succumb to the temptation to increase their take-home pay.

"People feel a certain hesitancy to cheat on an expense account until they realize how easy and acceptable it is," one middle manager from Minneapolis told me. "I think the reason for the hesitancy is the Puritan background of many American employees. They don't want to take something that they feel they haven't worked for. But the farther up the line you get in a company and the more you pad your expense account, the easier it becomes. And the higher you go, the less likely it is that your supervisors will question your account or not pay you for it.

"Even if the worker has certain moral reservations, there are many ways for him to assuage his conscience and continue to abuse the expense account. For example, a lot of guys will take a friend and his wife out to an expensive restaurant. They'll talk for a few minutes about putting together a merger or a contract or maybe the possibility of buying some company product. Then they spend the rest of the evening enjoying themselves. Getting free meals like this through the use of an expense account is a hidden form of compensation."

Although the prevailing attitudes may favor expense account abuse, the usual Christian approach to the issue is somewhat different. Take the case of a Christian journalism graduate named Jim, who decided that he wanted to work as a reporter on the West Coast. During his interviews with recruiters from several newspapers, he was introduced to the importance of the expense account as a part of the reporter's salary.

"We don't have any job openings here, but let me give you some advice about salaries," one job interviewer said. "The papers in _____ don't pay very high starting salaries, but they're quite liberal with their expense accounts. The _____ paper, on the other hand, has a relatively high starting salary, but it's rather tight on expenses. You'll have to see what kind of a starting salary each paper is willing to offer you. But to ascertain your total pay, be sure that you include what you'll be able to pocket in expenses."

Jim found that in the job he finally accepted, reporters were able to increase their salaried income by 10 to 15 percent through "creative" entries on their weekly expense account applications. A friend from the accounting department remarked during Jim's orientation period that "the hardest work some of our reporters do during the week is making out their expense account reports."

Some reporters would say that they took a political official out to lunch to discuss a story idea. Others would report that they took a cab to a remote section of town to investigate a tip on a reported homicide or a major accident. In most cases, of course, neither the lunches nor the news incidents ever occurred. The newspaper did not bother to conduct spot checks on any of the expense account entries. Nor did it require supporting documents unless certain individual amounts were excessively large or unless the total expense account exceeded the generally accepted limit of about 15 percent of the reporter's weekly salary. Finally, none of the reporters, as far as Jim was able to tell, reported their expense account windfalls to the Internal Revenue Service.

Jim was assigned to one of the paper's suburban offices, and it was there that he first confronted the practical workings of the expense account issue.

"I was told in no uncertain terms by some of the older reporters in that office that I was expected to put in at least twenty-five to thirty-five dollars each week in expenses," Jim confided. "They said that if I failed to put in for that much, I might either make trouble for the other reporters who were padding their accounts, or give my editors the impression I wasn't working very hard. I didn't know what to do at first."

These employees gave Jim the following written example of their typical weekly expense accounts. They told him to follow it generally, but to make certain alterations to eliminate obvious similarities with the accounts of other reporters:

Sunday—Phone calls	$1.30
Cab to police station and back	2.30
Monday—Phone calls	1.60
Cab to paper's police bureau and back	1.60
Cab to courthouse and back	2.10
Tuesday—Phone calls	1.40
Cab to police bureau and back	1.70
Cab to board of education and back	2.60
Wednesday—Phone calls	1.30
Cab to courthouse and back	2.60
Thursday—Phone calls	.90
Lunch with police detective involved in possibly newsworthy case	8.10
Cab to courthouse and back	2.40
TOTAL	$29.90

"All of these expense account entries would naturally be fictitious," Jim explained. "In spot news coverage, a reporter can almost always accomplish as much by telephone as he can by going over to see someone."

In resolving this expense account issue in a way that he felt was in harmony with his Christian convictions, Jim shifted his position several times.

"Before I took the job, I believed a person should make accurate entries on all written forms, including expense accounts," he said. "It was a matter of being honest, of not telling a lie.

"But the other workers on the paper said that, as a matter of custom, I was entitled to a certain amount of extra money each week under the cover of expenses. They explained that the company had made an allotment in its budget for that additional amount and that the money was sitting there each week, waiting for me to use it. They argued that I should put in for a cab even though I had actually taken a bus. Or I could legitimately list false entertainment expenses, such as meals that I had never paid for, to raise my expense account to the authorized weekly level of twenty-five or thirty-five dollars. In other words, I could skimp on my own comforts and pocket the difference in cash, instead of enjoying myself on the job with big lunches and cab rides. The only limitation was that, in depriving myself of certain expense account comforts, I should not do an unacceptable job in gathering news for the paper."

Jim protested at first that he didn't like the idea of taking money he had not earned. But one of his fellow workers replied, "Who's going to be the loser if you follow these customs? The company knows that we're doing this sort of thing, but the bosses just wink. They know that a certain amount of money has been allotted for expenses and that those expenses will be deductible at income tax time from the corporation's gross income. As for the federal government, there may not be any employees who report their additional expenses as taxable income. But if the government needs more money, it always compensates by raising taxes. In the final analysis we pay the Internal Revenue Service one way or another."

These arguments seemed convincing to Jim, and so he decided to follow the customs. He submitted expense accounts equal to the customary expense level by padding his report with entries for phony meals and cab rides. But after a few weeks, something didn't seem quite right.

"I knew it was wrong to say I had been to investigate fire alarms which had never occurred, or to claim I had eaten with people I didn't even know," he said. "How could I tell a person I was a Christian and at the same time be able to justify such obvious lies? But the extra money was attractive, and so I decided that, rather than fill out a completely honest expense account, I would compromise with custom. I resolved that I would no longer list completely false trips and meals. Instead, when it was convenient and would not hurt my news output, I would just stretch the truth a little and put in occasionally for a cab when I had actually traveled by bus."

But even this compromise failed ultimately to satisfy Jim. "I know that some Christians might be able to accommodate this 'cab-for-a-bus' compromise to their companies, but I was bothered about the moral inconsistencies. To my mind, there was still an element of hypocrisy there. I was praying during this period, and I looked through the Bible to find a solution. The answer was there in the Scriptures, of course, even though at the outset I didn't want to recognize it."

Jim said that there were three passages which were decisive in changing his approach to the expense account. First, he was struck by the contrast between the wise and the wicked servant in Matthew 24:45-51. The good servant was rewarded for properly executing his trust, but the bad fellow, who wasted his master's assets through poor management and excessive eating and drinking, was severely punished.

The second passage that impressed Jim was Paul's teaching in Ephesians 4:25-28. The apostle was quite explicit about being truthful and honest: "Therefore, putting away falsehood, let every one speak the truth with his neighbor, for we are members one of another. . . . Let the thief no longer steal, but rather let him labor, doing honest work with his hands. . . ."

But perhaps the most important passage for Jim—the one that he felt spoke directly to him on the expense account issue—was Proverbs 20:17: "Bread gained by deceit is sweet to a man, but afterward his mouth will be full of gravel."

"That's really how I felt, even after rejecting the most blatant kinds of cheating," he said. "My mouth, so to speak, was still full of gravel. I decided that the customs that everybody else was following were not for me. The other guys still argued that if I turned in an honest expense account, I'd get them in trouble with our editors just for the sake of making myself appear more moral than they were. But I knew it wasn't my honesty that would expose them to trouble—it was their cheating. Those customs just didn't seem to me to square with the teachings in the Bible and with my own conscience.

"Now, I no longer list expenses unless I have actually incurred them. And in spite of the fact that I have lost about fifteen hundred dollars in tax-free income a year, I've learned to get along quite easily without it. It was hard at first to give it up, but now I really don't miss it. I've found that the important thing, as far as expense accounts are concerned, is to keep my daily living consistent with my Christian faith and moral principles."

But what about the situation where you know you've incurred some expenses, but you can't remember exactly how much they were?

"I always try to keep exact records during the course of a week," Jim said. "It's true that sometimes I can't remember precisely how much money I spend on cabs or phones. Or I may have lost a luncheon receipt, and the exact amount, including the tip, may have slipped my mind. But in those situations, I don't get anxious. I usually have an idea of my approximate expenses, and so I estimate them as well as I can.

"If there's any area in which a customary company allocation for expenses comes into play, I think it's here. In other words, I feel that my company knows there is going to be a lack of precision when employees constantly move around from one assignment to the next, as newspaper reporters under deadline pressure have to do. As a result, when I can't remember a precise amount, I don't think that I have any duty to omit reporting the expense altogether. On the other hand, I have to fight an inclination to try to forget the precise amount so that I can pad my expense account with a clearer conscience."

The padded expense account is only one kind of customary fair stealing that the Christian will encounter at work. Pilfering of everything from paper clips and stamps on up to expensive retail merchandise is practiced in one form or another in most companies. Some bosses are tough in enforcing sanctions against offenders, but other supervisors just look the other way. Whatever the attitude of the employer, the Christian must always maintain his own standard —often defined by the question, "What would Christ do in this situation?" The ethical level of the company executives or of other co-workers cannot be the final word for the Christian. The ancient Hebrew code of conduct was unquestionably more demanding than any modern corporation's policies. Yet Jesus in his Sermon on the Mount called on us not to be satisfied even with the venerable Old Testament standards but to go beyond them both in our attitudes and in our deeds.

16
Kickbacks and Other Conflicts of Interest

In the race to make more money, workers sometimes do a little under-the-table dealing to gain an advantage over competitors. One of the most common ploys is to take the old success adage, "It's not what you know, but who you know," and go one step further: "It's not what or who you know, but how many conflicts of interest you can develop."

A conflict of interest can be defined generally as an unethical or illegal involvement by an individual in two or more different pursuits so that he is unable to discharge his appropriate responsibilities in one or more of those pursuits. On the surface, a worker's multiple commitments may seem innocent enough, but a closer inspection may reveal a serious conflict that compromises the employer's interests as well as the employee's integrity.

One simple example of a conflict of interest would be the judge who refuses to disqualify himself from hearing an antitrust case involving a corporation in which he holds a large amount of stock. He cannot be sufficiently objective in evaluating the position of the corporation, and so his performance as a judge must suffer. Another example of a conflict is the newspaperman who moonlights as the paid public-relations representative for an organization he is assigned by his editor to cover. The reporter in this situation may be benefiting financially from the arrangement, but his newspaper performance is compromised because of the interest he has in giving his P.R. employer a favorable public image.

The most common form of conflict of interest—one that is condoned in many sectors of our economy, especially among salesmen—is the kickback. In sales parlance, a kickback is an unauthorized rebate which is paid by a seller to a buyer to induce the buyer to purchase the seller's products. In New York and many other states, this practice is punishable as a crime called "commercial bribery." The New York statute prohibits any benefits to be paid to an employee, agent, or fiduciary of a company to influence that person's conduct on the job without the company's consent. Receiving a commercial bribe is also a crime and carries the same maximum misdemeanor penalty as offering the bribe—three months in jail and a five hundred dollar fine.

Kickbacks involve a conflict of interest in that the worker taking the bribe is induced to make business decisions because of the personal rewards he will receive rather than because of what is good for his company. In other words, he will probably throw business to the bribe-giver only on the basis of the bribe and not on the basis of how much better service the bribe-giver will render than his competitors. But because the kickback laws are rarely enforced against the small operator, it has become the general practice in many companies to break them without thinking twice about it.

The New Testament seems to refer to such business practices only indirectly, such as in parables and other teachings which encourage us to love our neighbors (employers) or to be true to trusts given to us by our superiors. (*See* Matthew 25:14-30.) But I'm convinced that God wants me to deal with other workers and employers on a straightforward, aboveboard basis, with company decisions being made on the merits and not because of some money or merchandise I may secretly give or receive.

I remember being offered a kickback once on a story I wrote while I was working as a newspaper reporter. An investigator for an attorney called me up and said his employer had just won an exceptionally high judgment in a civil lawsuit. He then said, "We'll remember you," and hung up the phone. Without knowing or caring what "remembering me" meant, I told my editor about the lawsuit, and we decided to go ahead and do a short story because of the intrinsic news value of the event.

A few days after the story ran in the paper, the same investigator called me again. I didn't recognize him at first, but he reminded me about the article.

"What's your address?" he asked.

"Why do you want to know?" I replied.

"Look, I appreciate your taking care of that story, and I'd like to send a little something to thank you."

Curious, I decided to find out what he meant. "What exactly are you thinking about sending me?" I asked.

"Oh, I had in mind a case of Scotch, good brand you know."

I then realized that he was talking in terms of a kickback worth seventy or eighty dollars just for that one story. And I also knew that our conversation had gone far enough.

"Look, I wrote that story because it was interesting and

worth the space, not because I want to get paid anything extra for it," I replied in as gentle a tone as I could muster under the circumstances. "Besides, I never take anything extra for writing a story, and so I really don't think there's any need for me to give you my address.

"Oh, okay, look, I didn't mean anything," he said, obviously flustered.

"Forget it, and thanks for the information about the lawsuit," I said.

In an obvious bribe attempt like this, I think the Christian's response should be firm and unwavering, but not self-righteous. I was in effect telling the guy, "My moral standards aren't the same as yours," and that statement comes uncomfortably close to the pietistic prayer of the Pharisee: " 'God, I thank thee that I am not like other men' " (Luke 18:11). Jesus condemned such pride by declaring ". . . every one who exalts himself will be humbled, but he who humbles himself will be exalted" (Luke 18:14). I have to make a special effort sometimes to remember that my own ethical potential is only as great as my commitment to Christ. My morality is not really "my" morality, but rather Christ living through me. And my moral responses are valid only to the degree that I submit my will to his.

Christians will find some variation of the kickback in almost any occupational field they choose. Even in the rarefied reaches of academe the kickback and its concomitant conflicts of interest threaten objectivity and responsibility. One Christian professor at a leading Eastern university said that book salesmen from numerous publishing companies frequently make appointments with him in an effort to push some line of texts.

"Sometimes, they make their sales pitch quite subtle," he said. "At other times, they'll come right out and say, 'I really want you to adopt my text, and if you do, I'll be happy to send you these books for your own use.' Free books benefit any teacher, of course, because everybody wants to build up his professional library. A typical faculty person probably adds a hundred books to his library this way, and if these are technical books, they cost a lot of money.

"The offer of these free books can induce a professor to order a text that might not be the best thing for the students. That's the danger. Plain and simple, it's a form of bribery. When I see that a salesman is coming on strong that way, I try to get rid of him quickly. I've often told salesmen, 'Look, you don't have any books that I'm interested in,' and they usually get the message fairly quickly and disappear. Sometimes I'll explain in detail why a book isn't right for my students, and that doesn't result in any special gifts either.

"When you're on a mailing list, the books will occasionally come in the mail without your having to talk to a salesman. I don't see any problem there. The problem for me comes when a salesman makes it known in a fairly obvious way that if you go along and adopt a particular book, there are certain favors that you'll receive. I think the main concern of the Christian teacher is to pick the right textbooks. My work, as well as my recreation, is supposed to be dedicated to God's purposes. That means that I do everything as though I'm doing it for him. If he's given me a responsibility for a class, I have to do the best job I possibly can, and that includes making the right choice of a textbook."

But kickbacks don't always present such clear-cut issues as those faced by this professor and myself. Take the customary annual gifts which are exchanged between business-men at Christmastime and which have nothing to do with any specific business deal. One traveling salesman who dealt mainly with large corporate customers said that tech-nically there was a rule in his company which prohibited any gifts, regardless of the time of year or the circumstances. "But the custom in the company at Christmas was that each salesman would give his customers some small gift. Often it was a bottle of liquor, and by any objective standard that was probably less of a bribe than treating a guy to a ten-or twelve-dollar lunch on your expense account. The com-pany executives know about this practice and have never tried to prohibit it.

"The reason for the rule against gifts is that once you give a small present, the inclination might be to give more—a watch or a suit of clothes or something. But in practice the big kickbacks come into play mainly when salesmen decide to bribe a purchasing agent in an effort to insure a specific sale. No one had a specific sale in mind at Christmas, just a remembrance of the relationship in general. These gifts are mainly regarded as tokens of appreciation and I myself see nothing wrong with them. I don't give liquor, but I've given a potted plant or something like that to a good customer at Christmas. That isn't a bribe in any sense of the word be-cause many of these people were my personal friends as well as my customers. And the company encouraged us to be friendly with our customers."

How the Christian handles a situation like this one de-pends both on his motives in giving and on the circum-stances surrounding each transaction. If the gift is offered out of a sense of goodwill and friendliness and is not intended in itself to influence the recipient to act in a particular way, then there may be nothing wrong with it. On the other hand, if the gift could be misconstrued, the Christian with even the purest motives may want to avoid the appearance of wrongdoing. When personal and business relationships become interwoven, the conflct-of-interest issue thus becomes more difficult to resolve. A satisfactory answer often requires considerable prayer and a conscientious analysis of where friendship ends and conflict of interest begins.

17
A Call to Full-Time Christian Service

The contemporary Christian faces moral challenges at work that sometimes make the problems of working people of a few decades ago appear to be child's play by comparison. Dishonesty and lethargy have plagued most societies, but we live in an age exceptional for its eroding values. The more technologically sophisticated we become, the less importance we seem to place on hard work and the pursuit of excellence. And a pervasive climate of moral permissiveness, of bending the rules whenever convenient, has spawned illegal schemes that have tainted the reputations of our highest leaders.

The Watergate affair stands as perhaps the worst scandal involving top government officials in our history. The public has become sickened and finally numb after hours of televised testimony by men who put expediency above morality, who were willing to commit crimes because "everybody else was doing it."

Nor has the business sector escaped the inexorable tide of corruption. Investigations of the highly regarded Equity Funding Corporation, for example, have disclosed an apparent conspiracy to concoct, computerize, and sell to other corporations millions of dollars in phony insurance policies. Things have become so bad that charges of cheating have even rocked that traditional bastion of innocence and right-eousness, the All-American Soapbox Derby. The 1973 national champion was stripped of his title because, at the urging of an adult relative, he allegedly raced and won with an illegal vehicle.

It's hard to find anyone to look up to anymore, and maybe, in the long run, that's a good thing. People are beginning to realize that if they want to maintain acceptable ethical standards on the job, they can't rely on other human beings to give them a value system. Some may argue, "Things are not worse now than in the past. People have always been dishonest. They've always cheated on their expense accounts and tax returns; accepted kickbacks; and stabbed their fellow workers in the back whenever possible. Every generation has its Teapot Dome, its indicted business executives and government officials."

All this may be true, but there seems to be a current tendency for people to be bolder in their rejection of traditional moral values. Cheating on the job used to be discussed, if at all, behind closed doors. But the greater openness today has been symbolically expressed through the character of Harry Stoner (played by Jack Lemmon) in the 1973 Paramount film, *Save the Tiger*. Stoner, a clothing manufacturer who lives in Beverly Hills, decides during a downturn in his business to cheat the Internal Revenue Service with falsified records, and finally, to burn down one of his buildings for the fire insurance proceeds. His reasoning: "There are no rules, only referees. And there's no room for losers." He also convinces his partner, Phil, that business crimes are sometimes necessary "to keep the people working" and "to meet the payroll." And, as far as we can tell from the movie, he gets away with his schemes.

Corruption is easier to accept or ignore when it stays underground. But the outright advocacy of cynicism and immorality provides a clear line for the Christian worker. We've reached an era when we either have to live our faith openly, or forget it. There's no middle ground, no haven for the secret Christian. Just as the crowing of the cock brought Peter back to reality and repentance after he had denied that he knew Jesus, so there is a cock crowing for us in the current scandals and open endorsements of immorality. If we compromise our values on the job, we countenance the moral decay and, in effect, deny that Christ lives in us.

But if we resolve to live and work a Christian life, we face a major obstacle at the outset: We've been brainwashed into believing that only certain individuals are called to full-time Christian service. Our ministers often make a special point of praising those who choose to become pastors or missionaries, but they give no recognition to individuals who pick retailing, law, or nursing. It's natural for a minister to be happy to welcome a young person into his own profession, just as it's natural for those in other fields to want to recruit bright young people. But such attitudes by pastors have encouraged church members to equate the ministry with full-time Christian service. The Christian layman often forgets or ignores the fact that *every* Christian is called to full-time Christian service.

In New Testament times many of the church leaders, such as the Apostle Paul, worked in secular professions in addition to their church positions. But our contemporary equivalents of the apostles—our evangelists, preachers, and heads of church denominations—are usually paid full salaries by their congregations or religious organizations. Their jobs are regarded as qualitatively different from the volunteer work done by church laymen. These so-called full-time Christians are sometimes even expected to receive a higher kind of call to their work than the rest of us. It's almost as though God is supposed to speak to church professionals through special signs or voices, but just pay partial attention to other Christians.

All such ideas are, of course, hogwash. God may speak to a pastor or bishop in a special way, but he's just as likely to communicate earth-shattering revelations to the lowliest layman in the most secular job. In fact, God seems almost more inclined to go to laymen when he has something important he wants done. This lay tradition pervades the Old Testament, as when God called Gideon away from his chores at a wine press to become a great military commander for Israel.

"Pray, Lord, how can I deliver Israel?" (Judges 6:15) Gideon protested. "Behold, my clan is the weakest in Manasseh, and I am the least in my family"(v.15). But the Lord replied simply, ". . . I will be with you"(v.16), and that was all it took for Gideon, the undistinguished layman, to succeed in one of God's most important tasks.

Nor is Gideon an isolated example. David started out as an ordinary shepherd, and with God's guidance he became the greatest king of ancient Israel. It's hard to find any apostle in the New Testament who wasn't also an ordinary workingman. Paul, the tentmaker, and Peter, the fisherman, are the two most obvious examples.

Because God is still calling laymen to do his work, we must learn to listen to him in our daily affairs. We should set aside any reservations about becoming too religious and prepare, if necessary, to follow in the footsteps of Gideon and David and the apostles. God has published an urgent want ad for mankind: HELP WANTED: FAITH REQUIRED. He has called each of us to enter a life of full-time Christian service by affirming that Jesus is Lord in our everyday work.